THE 10% LOW-FAT COOKBOOK

MIRIAM JACOBS

A Storey Publishing Book

STOREY

Storey Communications, Inc.
Schoolhouse Road
Pownal, Vermont 05261

DEDICATION

For two men who really knew about good food:
my father, Ton Jacobs,
and my brother, Ed Jacobs.

The mission of Storey Communications is to serve our customers by publishing practical information that encourages personal independence in harmony with the environment.

Edited by Pamela Lappies
Cover illustrations by Greg Imhoff
Cover and text design by Carol J. Jessop, Black Trout Design
Production by Faith E. Kaufman, Black Trout Design
Indexed by Sherri Dietrich

Printed in the United States by R.R. Donnelley
10 9 8 7 6 5 4 3 2 1

Library of Congress Cataloging-in-Publication Data

Jacobs, Miriam.
    10% low-fat cookbook / by Miriam Jacobs.
       p.   cm.
    "A Storey Publishing book."
    Includes index.
    ISBN 0-88266-855-2 (hbk. : alk. paper). — ISBN 0-88266-944-3 (pbk. : alk. paper)
    1. Low-fat diet — Recipes.   I. Title.
RM237.7.J33   1996
641.5'638—dc20
                                            96-26377
                                              CIP

TABLE OF CONTENTS

ACKNOWLEDGMENTS

A book is not created by one person, even though the author gets the credit.

From a technical standpoint, this book was created through the joint efforts of many creative and dedicated folks. Thank you to Pamela Lappies, who ably guided the manuscript through its editorial phases. Thank you to Dale Gelfand, who made it all sound like English, removed inconsistencies, patiently corrected this foreign-born woman's abominable spelling mistakes and in many other ways made this book sound good. Thank you to Carol Jessop for the interior design, which makes the recipes look edible even on a page.

On the home front, I could not have completed this project without the help of my fabulous immediate and extended family. I thank my younger children, Abigail and Adam, for patiently suffering through this project, even though it often meant eating foods not to their liking. Their words of encouragement ("I am sure *other* people will like it") sustained me! Thank you to Sarah, even though she is no longer living at home and therefore was not subjected to this barrage of food: It was her coming into my life that made me want to learn how to cook healthy food in the first place. Thank you to David Emblidge, who first encouraged me to write, and who is always willing to try a new food. He will see many of his great suggestions incorporated herein. His friendship with this family is a cornerstone in our lives. Thank you Elisa Novick and David Wade Smith for eating and eating and being so enthusiastic, and for all the computer time and help; this book would not have see the light without their generous help.

The final thank you is to my mom, Selma Jacobs, who fed us all so well for many years and who so very many years ago gave me the unglazed clay cooking pot I still use.

INTRODUCTION

This is a cookbook filled with nourishing, satisfying, delicious foods that derive ten percent or less of their calories from fat. It is not intended to be a diet book. I am not a doctor. I do not make recommendations about fat intake or endorse eating so little fat as a way of life. There are many opinions out there concerning the "right" percentage of fat to ingest. The government thinks that no more than thirty percent of our calories should come from fat, but some doctors, sports nutritionists, and other health professionals disagree. The only thing everybody *does* agree on is that, as a nation, we consume far too much fat—and that excess fat consumption has all sorts of scary implications for our health.

This book is intended to be a balancing tool for building an overall healthy diet. If you've eaten too much fat in a day or week, these delicious foods will get you back on track. These recipes are meant to become part of your repertory of meals. Use them once a week, three times a week, or every night. Call on this book to provide low-fat meals when you have overindulged, when you need something light, or when you want to avoid smothering your taste buds with fat. It will introduce you to new flavors, new techniques, and perhaps some new ingredients. And in the process you'll be eating foods that are lower in fat.

What Is Ten Percent or Less from Fat?

To measure our food, we start with calories. A calorie is the amount of heat required to bring one gram of water to one degree Celsius. What has that got to do with food? Heat production is a form of energy. When you eat food, its calories give you the heat or energy to do things. And when you eat more calories than you use up, the reserve is stored for you in the form of extra body weight.

From the standpoint of calories, there are three different types of nutrients in food: carbohydrates, proteins, and fats. These nutrients have unique chemical properties, which affect the numbers of calories they provide. A gram of carbohydrates and a gram of protein each supply us with four calories. A gram of fat, however, gives us nine calories. That's why a pound of pasta, which is almost completely carbohydrate, has fewer calories than a pound of butter, which is almost all fat.

To determine the percentage of calories we get from a nutrient in a particular food, we have to do some math. If a food has 90 calories and contains 1 gram of fat, then to figure calories from fat we must multiply 1 fat gram by 9, since a single fat gram provides 9 calories. Therefore 9 of those 90 calories come from fat. That's 10 percent right there, just from that 1 measly little gram!

When the numbers are easy like that, it isn't too hard. But when you're in the supermarket, face to face with a food that contains 315 calories and 8.2 grams of fat, it isn't immediately clear whether or not that food is high in fat. It would make things a lot simpler if the designers of the new food labels had included this information for us. The fastest way to estimate, when you don't happen to have a calculator handy, is to find the calories per serving, figure out what 10 percent of that number is, and compare the result to the calories from fat on the label. An easy way to get 10 percent of the calories is to move the decimal one place to the left. The resulting number is the highest number of calories that can come from fat. If the actual number of calories from fat on the label is larger, the food doesn't meet the 10-percent-or-less criterion.

I could not have written this cookbook without my computer program, which calculated ingredients and calories instantly. The ability to input a new ingredient and instantly see how it would affect the percentage of calories from fat was wonderful. If you are truly serious about tracking fat grams in recipes and you have a computer at your disposal, I highly recommend that you investigate the available programs.

Quick and Easy 10% Formula

If you're in the grocery store without your calculator, and you're lousy at math, don't give up. Here's a way to know at a glance whether something fits the 10%-of-its-calories-from-fat requirement.

1. Locate the nutrition label. Find the <u>calories</u> per serving and the <u>calories from fat</u> per serving.

Amount per serving	
Calories	230
Calories from fat	20

2. Move the decimal of the <u>calories</u> per serving one place to the left. (In the example above, 230 becomes 23.0.)

3. Is the number you get after moving the decimal LARGER than the number of <u>calories from fat</u>? If the answer is YES, this food gets LESS than 10 percent of its calories from fat. (In the example, the answer is YES because 23.0 is larger than 20.)

   • YES = LESS than 10% calories from fat
   • NO = MORE than 10% calories from fat

Exact 10% Formula

To find the exact percentage of calories from fat, multiply the fat grams by nine and divide by the number of calories.

$$\frac{\text{FAT GRAMS} \times 9}{\text{NUMBER OF CALORIES}} \times 100 = \text{PERCENTAGE OF CALORIES FROM FAT}$$

Techniques

How you prepare food can be one of the most significant ways to control fat content. Traditional methods, such as sautéing and deep frying, use liberal quantities of fat, causing the percentage of calories from fat to climb sky-high. There are alternatives, however, that will cut the fat and boost the flavor.

Sauces. You'll notice that I've included many creamy sauces in this book. Using sauces is a great way to make foods satisfying. I don't make these sauces in the classic manner, of course, because that would include lots of butter and possibly cream, as well. Instead, I use a technique that I learned more than a decade ago from the first Pritikin cookbook, and I thank the good doctor for the brilliant breakthrough.

Sautéing in broth. I also learned from the Pritikin cookbooks to place food in nonstick cookware and sauté using broth instead of oil or butter, a technique I continue to use extensively.

Cooking spray. Another good way to cut fat is to use nonstick cooking spray. Cooking spray does, in fact, contain a trace amount of fat, but it's too small to make a difference. Using cooking spray lets you "fry" food without adding considerable fat.

Fresh ingredients. Using herbs, spices, fruits, and vegetables at their peak of flavor does a lot to compensate for the flavor the missing fat would have supplied.

Unglazed clay-pot roasting. This is an ancient cooking technique: The Roman gourmand Lucullus cooked his dishes in water-soaked unglazed pottery well over two thousand years ago. Using the clay-pot method of roasting food is an excellent way to reduce fat without sacrificing taste. In fact, clay pots can't work their magic if fat is present. When foods roast together in the soaked clay, their flavors blend in ways just not possible using conventional methods.

As with any new equipment, if you have never used a pot like this, read the instructions. You must soak the pot in water for fifteen minutes before putting food into it. Once the food is in the pot, place it into a cold oven and *then* turn on the heat; putting the soaked clay into a hot oven will break the pot. As it heats, the water-soaked clay produces steam, which will create heights in flavor not otherwise possible.

Nonstick cookware. A good set of set of nonstick pans is a must in your arsenal of low-fat implements. In almost any other pan, your food will stick unless you use fat. The new breed of nonstick cookware will last for quite a while, even if you don't always use wooden or plastic utensils. Once the surface starts to deteriorate, discard them. Also worth considering are the stainless-steel pans with carbon centers and lids that fit so precisely, you can employ the "waterless" method of cooking.

Special Foods

While I've generally included ingredients that are widely available, I've also made use of a few products that are found primarily at larger supermarkets or health-food stores. Using them stretches the possibilities of low-fat cooking, making the extra effort to find them worth it.

Vegetable-broth mix. To add flavor to a dish—a constant challenge when you cut out fat—vegetable broth can't be beat. Brands and varieties abound in liquid, powdered, and cubed versions. And you can choose other flavors, such as chicken and beef. My requirements (you may feel differently) are that it has to be fat-free—and not all of them are—and it can't contain MSG or various other chemicals. I used a powdered mix, one heaping teaspoon of which flavors a cup of water.

Pasteurized dried egg whites. This product has been available to the commercial industry for a long time, and now it's available to the consumer. It looks like superfine flour. The miracle is that it whips up just like fresh egg whites, so you don't have to throw away all those yolks when you want to avoid their high fat content. A table on the back of the can shows you how much product and water you need to mix to get the equivalent of the egg whites you're trying to replace. Being shelf stable, it needs no refrigeration. The only brand that I know is Just Whites. Ask for it at a specialty store. If they don't carry it, they'll probably be able to order it.

Soy meat substitutes. Most people who want to use soy meat products are concerned with maintaining a vegetarian diet, not with eating low-fat foods. Consequently, many soy meat substitutes are not particularly low in fat. However, brands do exist that *are* low in fat and have an excellent meaty flavor. The brand I generally use, Gimme Lean, has no calories from fat, and in this book the nutritional calculations that follow each recipe are based on that product. (A related but very different product is texturized vegetable protein, or TVP, as it's often called. TVP is not included in these recipes, principally because of its unappetizing appearance, which resembles kibble. The soy meat substitute called for in these recipes has the texture and consistency of link sausage.)

By using the right techniques and ingredients, low-fat cooking can be easier than you might have assumed. After you've used the recipes here and become familiar with the methods designed to keep fat to a minimum, adapt them to your own recipes.

CHAPTER 1

APPETIZERS

Traditionally, when meals consisted of many fat-laden courses, appetizers were meant spark the appetite, to coax the diners to feel enthusiastic about eating. It's a cause I find hard to embrace. My appetite tends to be sharp enough as it is! But today we have a new need and use for these little dishes, because appetizers can be a great ally to cutting fat intake. These foods really do belong at the beginning of an elaborate, festive meal. The appetizer course adds to the anticipation of more food to come, and, since it prolongs the meal, allows for more leisurely conversation and pleasant time spent with friends.

Everyday meals can also benefit from having a quick appetizer served. Since meals will feel more filling and elaborate, your temptation to cheat will be lessened. The illusion of plenty created by an extra course can help you overcome the craving for something more.

Many of these foods will also satisfy you in the late afternoon and the late evening, when your energy is low and you crave something to eat. It's good to prepare for munchie attacks: Always have something around that will be good to eat but won't blow your plans to keep fat at a minimum.

Having dips and spreads handy to serve with raw vegetables or to spread on bread will keep you on track. The idea is to strategize and make appetizers during an extra minute so that they'll be instantly on hand when you're hungry. It might work for you always to have one variety of yogurt cheese prepared to spread on pita bread. I know a family whose standard snack is salsa and no-fat tortilla chips. Salsa is easy to make, and it keeps well.

Finally, appetizers are good party fare. The Black Bean Dip and Caponata are personal favorites, and to judge by their remarks, friends and family agree. Dips and spreads, with raw vegetables, no-fat chips, pita bread, and baguettes, round out the party fare. All can be made ahead of time, letting you enjoy the festivities, and not blow your low-fat plans or those of your guests.

Artichoke Dip

This delicate dip is good with pita wedges or mild raw vegetables such as sweet red peppers and carrots. I was fortunate enough to have a few spoonfuls left over, so I made a delicious sandwich with it, adding just a slice of tomato.

6 artichoke hearts, canned
$\frac{2}{3}$ cup nonfat sour cream
1 teaspoon lemon juice
2 teaspoons minced shallot
1 teaspoon minced fresh dill
Salt and freshly ground black pepper

1. Drain the artichoke hearts. Place them in a blender, adding the sour cream, lemon juice, shallot, dill, and salt and pepper to taste.
2. Blend until smooth, scraping down the sides as necessary.
3. Refrigerate and serve.

4 SERVINGS
PER SERVING: 105 Calories • 0.2 Gram Fat • 1.7% Calories from Fat

Black Bean Dip

Even people who tend to avoid bean dishes give this recipe uniform and loud raves. You can make the dip hotter by adding chili powder or very small amounts of cayenne, and it can easily be doubled for parties and potlucks. Serve with fat-free tortilla chips or fresh veggies. If you don't have black beans on hand, kidney beans can be substituted.

1 can (12 ounces) black beans
1 small onion, cut into chunks
2 garlic cloves, minced
$\frac{1}{3}$ cup tomato paste

Juice of 1 large lemon
1 teaspoon chili powder
$\frac{1}{2}$ teaspoon ground cumin
$\frac{1}{3}$ cup chopped fresh cilantro

1. Drain the black beans.
2. Place the onion, garlic, tomato paste, lemon juice, chili powder, cumin, and cilantro in a food processor or blender and process until fairly smooth. Add the beans and process again until smooth but still slightly chunky.

8 SERVINGS
PER SERVING: 166 Calories • 0.9 Gram Fat • 4.6% Calories from Fat

Crab Dip

This luxurious dip can be doubled for larger gatherings. It's also great on French bread, cut lengthwise, with tomato slices and lettuce.

$\frac{3}{4}$ cup nonfat sour cream
$\frac{1}{4}$ cup nonfat mayonnaise
1 teaspoon prepared horseradish
$\frac{1}{4}$ teaspoon dry mustard
$\frac{1}{2}$ teaspoon low-sodium soy sauce

Dash hot sauce
Pinch of cayenne
$\frac{1}{4}$ pound crabmeat
Salt and freshly ground black pepper

1. Combine the sour cream and mayonnaise in a medium bowl and mix well. Add the horseradish, dry mustard, soy sauce, hot sauce, and cayenne and mix well again. Add crabmeat and stir to combine.
2. Chill for 2 hours to let the flavors blend.

4 SERVINGS
PER SERVING: 82 Calories • 0.2 Gram Fat • 2.5% Calories from Fat

Seviche

Immersing scallops in lime juice gives the impression that they've been cooked. Make sure that the scallops are sushi quality and absolutely fresh. If you don't have a reputable fishmonger or you have any doubt at all about the quality of the scallops, prepare them in another manner.

1 pound sushi-quality scallops
Juice of 5 limes
Cayenne
$\frac{1}{4}$ cup minced Vidalia onion
$\frac{1}{4}$ cup minced fresh cilantro
1 large tomato, chopped

1. Cut the scallops in half, or thirds if they're very large, and cover with the lime juice and a pinch of cayenne. Cover and let the scallops marinate in the refrigerator for 4 hours.
2. Toss together the onion, cilantro, tomato, and another pinch of cayenne. Arrange the salad on a serving plate. Drain the scallops and arrange over the salad.

4 SERVINGS
PER SERVING: 138 Calories • 1.3 Grams Fat • 7.6% Calories from Fat

Yogurt Cheese

There are quite a few no-fat dairy products on the market, but I dislike the taste of most of them. Creamy, dense yogurt cheese tastes good, contains no questionable ingredients, and is a great base from which to make spreads. Use vanilla-flavored nonfat yogurt for a sweet spread.

2 cups nonfat plain yogurt

1. Line a sieve with 2 layers of large basket-type coffee filters. Set the sieve over a mixing bowl, making sure that there's at least an inch between the bottom of the sieve and the bowl. Carefully scoop the yogurt into the coffee filters. If there seems to be a little too much yogurt, heap it up in the middle. Cover loosely with a piece of plastic wrap. Place the covered sieve with the yogurt and the bowl in the refrigerator and leave for 24 to 36 hours. Pour out the accumulated whey occasionally.

2. When you've poured out a total of about ¾ cup of whey and the cheese is firm, invert the cheese on a plate. Peel off and discard the filters. Store the yogurt cheese in a closed container. You'll have a little over a cup of yogurt cheese, but the final quantity will depend on how liquid the yogurt was and how long you let it drip.

1 RECIPE
PER RECIPE: 253 Calories • 0.8 Gram Fat • 2.9% Calories from Fat

Italian Yogurt Cheese

Spread this on a bagel, with a slice of ripe tomato.
It's the perfect accompaniment to a bowl of Celery Corn Chowder or Minestrone.

1 cup yogurt cheese (see above)
1 teaspoon vegetable-broth mix
1 teaspoon minced shallot
1 teaspoon minced fresh oregano
½ teaspoon minced fresh thyme
Salt and freshly ground pepper

1. Mix all the ingredients well.
2. Chill, letting the flavors blend for an hour. Serve cold.

4 SERVINGS
PER SERVING: 37 Calories • 0.1 Gram Fat • 3.1% Calories from Fat

Vegetable Yogurt Cheese

Yogurt cheeses can be used in a wide variety of ways. Besides being excellent as a dip with raw vegetables, they make good sandwich spreads, enhance flavor when added to a soup right before serving, and spice up a baked potato—all with very little fat.

2 sun-dried tomatoes
1 cup yogurt cheese (page 8)
1 teaspoon vegetable-broth mix
1 tablespoon minced fresh basil
$\frac{1}{4}$ cup minced fresh parsley
Salt and freshly ground black pepper

1. Pour some boiling water into a cup and add the sun-dried tomatoes. Let them soften for 5 minutes. Drain and finely chop.

2. Combine the tomatoes with the yogurt cheese, broth mix, basil, parsley, and salt and pepper to taste. Let the flavors blend for an hour before serving.

4 SERVINGS
PER SERVING: 107 Calories • 0.9 Gram Fat • 7.0% Calories from Fat

Tomato Cilantro Salsa

There are some good low-fat salsas out there, but nothing compares with fresh. Be sure to serve this salsa with fat-free tortilla chips. Wear rubber gloves when cutting up hot peppers to keep their irritating juices off your skin. You can double or triple this recipe, adjusting the heat with hot sauce.

$\frac{1}{2}$ jalapeño pepper
3 plum tomatoes, diced
$\frac{1}{3}$ cup diced green pepper
1 scallion, minced
3 tablespoons minced fresh cilantro
2 teaspoons fresh lemon juice
Hot sauce

1. Cut the jalapeño pepper in half and remove all the seeds and the white membrane. Mince the pepper.

2. In a small bowl combine all the ingredients, adding hot sauce to taste, and mix well. Serve cold.

1 RECIPE
PER RECIPE: 103 Calories • 1.4 Grams Fat • 10.0% Calories from Fat

Tomatillo Salsa

This is a very mild salsa: Roasted poblano peppers are not very hot, and the tomatillos are pleasantly tart. If you like your salsa with more zip, add some hot sauce, chili pepper, or pinches of cayenne.

8 medium tomatillos
1 poblano pepper
$\frac{1}{4}$ cup chopped red onion
$\frac{1}{4}$ teaspoon vegetable-broth mix
$\frac{1}{4}$ cup water
$\frac{1}{8}$ teaspoon lemon juice
3 tablespoons minced fresh cilantro
4 cups nonfat tortilla chips

1. Preheat the broiler. Have a brown paper bag ready.
2. Place the poblano pepper 6 inches under the broiler and char it without burning. Rotate the pepper after about 6 minutes and continue to turn and blacken all sides. Use wooden spoons to turn the pepper, taking great care not to pierce it. When all sides are done, place the pepper immediately in the brown bag and let it cool for 10 minutes. The steam released in the bag will help to loosen the skin.
3. Remove the pepper from the bag and slip off the skin. Cut off the stem, remove the seeds, and chop the pepper.
4. Slip off the papery husks from the tomatillos and quarter them. In a medium-size saucepan, combine the tomatillos, pepper, onion, broth mix, water, and lemon juice. Bring the mixture to a boil and then reduce the heat and let it simmer for 15 minutes.
5. When the mixture has cooled, blend in the cilantro. Serve at room temperature or chill and serve cold.

8 SERVINGS
PER RECIPE: 482 Calories • 4.6 Grams Fat • 8.7% Calories from Fat

Onion Relish and Spread

This dish was nearly polished off by my testers before it even got to the table! Nobody guessed that the secret ingredient was prunes—and depending on your family's feelings about this sweet and useful fruit, you might not wish to tell them. Serve with pita bread or on baguettes.

2 medium onions	$\frac{1}{2}$ teaspoon paprika
1 large tomato	$\frac{1}{4}$ teaspoon dry mustard
12 prunes	$\frac{1}{4}$ teaspoon vinegar
1 teaspoon tamari soy sauce	

1. Slice the onions into medium-thick rings. Cut the rings in half to make half circles. Chop the tomatoes. Cut the prunes into six pieces. (Kitchen scissors work well.)

2. Place all the ingredients in a nonstick skillet and bring to a simmer. Stir, cover, and let simmer gently for 45 minutes. Stir occasionally, mashing the ingredients together. If the mixture becomes too dry, add a little water, but you want to end up with a relatively stiff paste.

3. Serve hot, warm, or cool.

4 SERVINGS
PER SERVING: 74 Calories • 0.3 Gram Fat • 3.7% Calories from Fat

Apple Cranberry Chutney

Chutney is a great accompaniment to a Thanksgiving turkey, but it also tastes wonderful the rest of the year on turkey sandwiches. Once assembled, all you have to do is let it simmer.

1 cup cranberries	$\frac{1}{2}$ teaspoon ginger, dried
2 Granny Smith apples, chopped	$\frac{1}{4}$ teaspoon mace
1 medium onion, chopped	$\frac{1}{4}$ teaspoon ground cardamom
2 garlic cloves, minced	$\frac{1}{2}$ teaspoon ground cumin
1 lemon	$\frac{1}{4}$ teaspoon dry mustard
$\frac{1}{4}$ cup apple cider vinegar	1 tablespoon honey
1 teaspoon ground coriander	$\frac{1}{3}$ cup currants

1. Place all the ingredients in a medium-size saucepan in the order listed. Stir and bring to a boil.

2. Reduce the heat and simmer for 30 minutes. Serve at room temperature.

ABOUT 2 CUPS
PER RECIPE: 447 Calories • 1.6 Grams Fat • 2.8% Calories from Fat

Baguettes with Roasted Garlic and Tomatoes

Once garlic is roasted it loses its bite, and what remains is a sweet but heady taste. The roasted heads keep well for a few days when refrigerated in a closed container, so while you're at it, you might want to roast several heads at once. However, for peak taste, let them warm to room temperature before serving. Be sure the tomatoes are drop-dead ripe and full of flavor; otherwise skip them, and just eat the bread and garlic.

4 garlic heads
1 baguette
2 tomatoes, sliced
Salt and freshly ground black pepper

1. Preheat the oven to 400°F. Place the whole garlic heads in a baking bowl and bake for 45 minutes. Cool, then break apart into individual cloves.

2. Cut the baguette into slices. Squeeze a clove of buttery soft garlic onto each slice and top with a slice of tomato. Add salt and pepper to taste.

4 SERVINGS
PER SERVING: 326 Calories • 3.6 Grams Fat • 10.0% Calories from Fat

Caponata

I prefer this classic Italian dish to its cousin ratatouille because of the sweetness of the currants and the bite of the vinegar. But if you disagree, omit those ingredients and you'll have this eggplant dish the way the French do. Serve it with pita bread or crackers.

1 medium eggplant
1 medium onion
6 garlic cloves
1 can (28 ounces) crushed tomatoes
$\frac{2}{3}$ cup currants
$\frac{1}{4}$ cup plus 1 tablespoon minced fresh basil

1 tablespoon minced fresh oregano
(or 1 teaspoon dried)
$\frac{1}{2}$ teaspoon salt
2 teaspoons cider vinegar
$\frac{1}{2}$ teaspoon freshly ground black pepper

1. Dice the eggplant into ½-inch cubes. Finely chop the onion and mince the garlic. Combine them in a large pot with the tomatoes, currants, 1 tablespoon of the basil, oregano, salt, vinegar, and pepper. Simmer uncovered for 2 hours, stirring occasionally to prevent scorching.

2. Serve at room temperature, with the remaining basil sprinkled on top.

8 SERVINGS
PER SERVING: 74 Calories • 0.5 Gram Fat • 5.2% Calories from Fat

Chinese Dumplings

I was testing this dish just as my son, Adam, was having a birthday party. Adults and young men alike gave these dumplings top honors! Though making dumplings is a bit time-consuming, the praise and smiles are worth the extra effort.

4 leaves romaine lettuce
3 scallions
6 ounces sausage-flavored soy meat substitute
4 tablespoons plus 2 teaspoons tamari soy sauce
1 celery stalk, minced
12 wonton wrappers

1. Wash and dry the romaine leaves and arrange them on individual serving plates. Mince 1 of the scallions, using green and white parts.

2. To make the dumplings, brown the "sausage meat" in a nonstick skillet, stirring continuously. Add 2 teaspoons of the soy sauce, the minced scallion, and the minced celery. Cook for 3 minutes.

3. On a cutting board, moisten the edges of a wonton wrapper with water, using a pastry brush. Place a small amount of the sautéed mixture in the center of the wrapper and fold the wrapper over to form a triangle, pressing the edges together so they'll stick. Continue with the rest of the wrappers and filling. Let the dumplings rest for 15 minutes.

4. To make the dipping sauce, mince the remaining 2 scallions and combine with the remaining 4 tablespoons of soy sauce. Pour into small bowls for serving.

5. Bring a large pot of water to a rolling boil. Gently lower the dumplings into the boiling water and cook for 4 minutes. Remove and serve immediately on the lettuce, with dipping sauce.

12 SERVINGS
PER SERVING: 219 Calories • 1.4 Grams Fat • 5.7% Calories from Fat

Red Pepper Scallion Fritatta

As you undoubtedly know by now, the fat calories in eggs are in the yolks. In this dish, even a single yolk would cause the calories from fat to increase nearly ten times! Turmeric will give the pasteurized dried egg whites a sunny yellow color, and the vegetables and seasonings will add flavor.

2 tablespoons water
1 cup finely chopped red pepper
2 scallions, finely chopped
6 egg whites (or $\frac{1}{4}$ cup pasteurized dried egg whites plus $\frac{3}{4}$ cup water)
2 tablespoons skim milk
1 teaspoon Dijon mustard
$\frac{1}{4}$ teaspoon ground turmeric
$\frac{1}{4}$ teapoon salt
1 cup finely chopped, cooked potato
Pinch of paprika

1. Preheat the broiler. In an ovenproof, nonstick skillet, heat the water. Add the pepper and scallions and simmer for 5 minutes.
2. In a mixing bowl, whip the egg whites (or pasteurized dried egg whites and water) until frothy. Add the milk, mustard, turmeric, and salt.
3. When the pepper and scallions are soft and the water has evaporated, scatter the potatoes over the bottom of the pan and pour the egg mixture on top. Cover and cook over a low heat for 8 minutes, or until most of the egg has set.
4. Sprinkle the paprika over the frittata and place under the broiler until the top has some color. Check it every 30 seconds to avoid charring.

2 SERVINGS
PER SERVING: 100 Calories • 0.3 Gram Fat • 2.9% Calories from Fat

CHAPTER 2

SOUPS, SALADS, AND BREADS

Soups, salads, and breads are no longer just components of seven-course meals. They're the ideal meal for a family on the run. A note that says "Soup is on the stove, salad and bread on the counter. Help yourself!" is often the sum total of dinnertime "conversation" when games and rehearsals and meetings have everybody on the run.

With the exception of soups relying on cream, most broth varieties are naturally low in fat. Refrigerating any soup will cause the fat to congeal on top, making it simple to remove. Soup can also fit into busy schedules, since it can be made ahead of time without sacrificing taste. Start a pot of soup simmering while you're cleaning up from dinner and doing the dishes. By the time you finish, tomorrow's dinner can already be done! Many of the soups I've included are hearty and filling, with beans and root vegetables. Not much more is needed for a complete meal.

Salads are often naturally low in fat, but dressings generally are not, so make sure you have low- and no-fat varieties on hand. There are commercial no-fat dressings available that use ingredients and techniques too cumbersome to prepare at home, so I suggest you experiment and find some you like in addition to the few I offer.

Breads, too, are often low in fat, but most spreads and dressings are not. I find most of the no-fat dairy products unpalatable if eaten straight. For spreads, consider using some of the recipes for dips and yogurt cheese in the Appetizer chapter, or make up your own. I've offered a few variations, but possibilities for both savory and sweet spreads from yogurt cheese are endless.

SOUPS

Though these recipes give specific ingredients and quantities, they can easily be adapted to create soups that use up leftovers. A few boiled potatoes, steamed green beans, or a half cup of chicken can find their way into a pot of soup and meet with raves from all your hungry guests.

A hearty, steaming bowl of soup, a fresh salad, and hot scones from the oven: It's difficult to see what "sacrifice" you're making with such a meal!

Acorn Squash Tomato Soup

This autumn soup is best served piping hot and would be great with some Corny Dill Corn Bread (page 49). It also gives you a substantial portion of your daily vitamin A requirement.

1 medium acorn squash	$\frac{1}{2}$ teaspoon freshly ground black pepper
3 cups tomato juice	$1\frac{1}{2}$ cups frozen corn
1 tablespoon dried minced onion	2 tablespoons chopped fresh parsley

1. Preheat the oven to 400°F. Cut the acorn squash in half and scoop out the seeds. Place the squash cut side down in a baking dish filled with an inch of water. Place in the oven for 30 minutes, or until the squash can be easily pierced with a sharp knife. Let cool.

2. Scoop the flesh into a food processor or blender. Add the tomato juice, onion, and pepper and process until very smooth. Place the purée in a medium-size saucepan.

3. Add the corn to the puree and heat through until boiling. Reduce the heat and simmer for 5 minutes. Sprinkle with the parsley and serve.

4 SERVINGS
PER SERVING: 124 Calories • 0.8 Gram Fat • 4.7% Calories from Fat

Celery Corn Chowder

There are certain chilly nights in late summer when a hot bowl of soup sounds appealing, and this is the one to have. Although you can make it at other times of the year with frozen corn, you'll be glad you went to the trouble of scraping the corn kernels off the cob when you taste this concoction.

1 cup nonfat chicken broth
1 cup skim milk
$\frac{1}{4}$ cup flour
$\frac{1}{2}$ teaspoon salt
$\frac{3}{4}$ teaspoon fresh minced thyme (or $\frac{1}{4}$ teaspoon dried)
$\frac{1}{4}$ teaspoon freshly ground black pepper
1 teaspoon snipped fresh dill
2 cups fresh corn kernels
1 cup chopped celery
Freshly ground black pepper

1. Place the broth, milk, flour, and salt into a food processor or blender. Heat a nonstick skillet for 30 seconds. Blend the milk mixture and pour into the hot pan. Stirring constantly, heat the sauce until it thickens.

2. Add the thyme, pepper, dill, corn, and celery. Simmer over low heat for 15 minutes, stirring occasionally. Serve hot with pepper to taste ground on the top.

4 SERVINGS
PER SERVING: 203 Calories • 1.5 Grams Fat • 6.0% Calories from Fat

Chicken Soup

I'm a purist about chicken soup—I like it without vegetables. If you like vegetables in yours, add fresh ones after discarding the ones used for broth. After two hours of cooking, the carrot and onion have lost their flavor to the broth.

10 ounces skinless chicken breast halves, bone in
1 medium carrot
$\frac{1}{4}$ cup fresh parsley sprigs plus 1 tablespoon minced
1 medium onion

8 whole peppercorns
1 bay leaf
6 cups water

1. Combine all the ingredients except the minced parsley in a large saucepan and simmer for 2 hours.
2. Strain the broth and discard the vegetables. Let the chicken pieces cool, remove any meat that remains on the bones, and discard the bones. Cut the chicken into bite-size pieces and return the chicken to the broth. Refrigerate until cooled.
3. When you're ready to serve, skim the congealed chicken fat from the top. Reheat and pour into serving bowls. Sprinkle minced parsley on top just before serving.

4 SERVINGS
PER SERVING: 118 Calories • 1.3 Grams Fat • 9.4% Calories from Fat

Creamed Broccoli Soup

This is a lighter version of the usual creamed broccoli soups, but the same homespun goodness will warm your belly and soul.

1 head broccoli
4 scallions
1 large potato
3 cups water

$1\frac{1}{2}$ teaspoons minced fresh rosemary
(or $\frac{1}{2}$ teaspoon dried)
$\frac{1}{4}$ teaspoon chili powder
Salt and freshly ground black pepper

1. Trim the florets from the broccoli. Peel the broccoli stalks and cut into 1-inch pieces. Cut the scallions and potato into chunks. Pour the water into a medium-size saucepan and add the broccoli, scallions, potato, rosemary, and chili powder. Bring to a rolling boil, stir, reduce the heat, and simmer for 30 minutes, or until the potato chunks are very soft. Remove from the heat and let cool slightly.
2. Pour the soup into a food processor or blender in batches and purée, adding salt and pepper to taste. Reheat and serve very hot.

4 SERVINGS
PER SERVING: 30 Calories • 0.2 Gram Fat • 4.9% Calories from Fat

Curried Cauliflower Soup

This deep yellow, creamy, aromatic soup will make your house smell irresistible—and your mouth rejoice.

1 cauliflower head	$\frac{1}{2}$ teaspoon ground coriander
2 medium potatoes	$\frac{1}{8}$ teaspoon ground cinnamon
1 medium onion	1 teaspoon ground turmeric
3 cups water	$\frac{1}{2}$ teaspoon salt
1 teaspoon ground cumin	$\frac{1}{8}$ teaspoon cayenne

1. Cut the cauliflower into florets. Slice the potatoes into ½-inch cubes, and mince the onion. Combine with the water, cumin, coriander, cinnamon, turmeric, salt, and cayenne in a soup pot and simmer for 30 minutes. Cool the soup slightly.

2. Puree half of the soup in a food processor or blender and add it back to the soup. Heat through and serve hot.

4 SERVINGS
PER SERVING: 47 Calories • 0.3 Gram Fat • 5.0% Calories from Fat

Dutch Split-Pea Soup

For hundreds of years split-pea soup has been served in the Netherlands from stalls erected at the edge of the canals to skaters in need of sustenance and warmth. The original versions add prodigious amounts of fat; this low-fat adaptation will nonetheless warm you down to the very last frozen toe.

2 cups split peas	8 cups water
2 large onions, chopped	1 tablespoon low-sodium soy sauce
6 garlic cloves, minced	1 teaspoon dried basil
2 carrots, sliced	$\frac{1}{4}$ teaspoon cayenne
2 bay leaves	

1. Combine the peas, onions, garlic, carrots, bay leaves, water, soy sauce, basil, and cayenne in a large pot and simmer on very low heat for 2 hours.

2. Add salt and pepper to taste and serve hot.

6 SERVINGS
PER SERVING: 251 Calories • 0.9 Gram Fat • 3.2% Calories from Fat

Garbanzo Tomato Soup with Basil

This light soup, to begin a meal, delights the palate with the rich flavor of ripe tomatoes.

3 large ripe tomatoes
1 cup nonfat chicken broth
2 tablespoons chopped fresh basil
$\frac{3}{4}$ cup canned chickpeas, drained
2 tablespoons minced fresh cilantro

1. Bring a large saucepan of water to a boil. Add the tomatoes and let boil for 1 minute. Plunge the tomatoes into ice-cold water; the skins should burst. When the tomatoes have cooled slightly, remove and slip off the skins. Chop into a few pieces.
2. Combine the tomatoes, broth, and basil in a blender and process until smooth.
3. Pour the tomato broth into a saucepan, add the chickpeas, and bring to a boil. Simmer for 10 minutes. Serve hot with cilantro sprinkled on top.

4 SERVINGS
PER SERVING: 76 Calories • 0.8 Gram Fat • 9.2% Calories from Fat

Spinach Bean Soup

You will make this again and again because it's easy, tasty, and terrifically nutritious. It offers a substantial amount of vitamins A and C as well as plenty of calcium and iron.

2 cups water
1 package (10 ounces) frozen spinach
1 medium onion, chopped
2 garlic cloves, minced
1 teaspoon low-sodium soy sauce
1 teaspoon vegetable-broth mix
$\frac{3}{4}$ teaspoon minced fresh thyme
(or $\frac{1}{4}$ teaspoon dried)
1 can (15$\frac{1}{2}$ ounces) white beans, drained
Salt and freshly ground black pepper

1. In a medium-size saucepan, heat the water to a boil. Add the spinach, onion, garlic, soy sauce, broth mix, and thyme. Simmer for 10 minutes, or until the onion is soft.
2. Transfer half the spinach and broth to a blender and process until smooth. Pour the puree back into the soup. Add the beans and salt and pepper to taste. Heat through.

6 SERVINGS
PER SERVING: 264 Calories • 0.8 Gram Fat • 2.6% Calories from Fat

Indian Lentil Soup

This is a very easy, delicious, and thick soup. The taste is quite convincingly Indian, and it freezes well.

6 cups water
1 pound lentils
1 medium plus 1 small onion, chopped
2 garlic cloves, minced
1 bay leaf
2 teaspoons ground cumin
2 carrots
1 medium sweet red pepper
2 teaspoons cider vinegar
1 teaspoon ground ginger
$\frac{1}{4}$ teaspoon ground cinnamon
$\frac{1}{4}$ teaspoon cayenne

1. Bring the water to a boil in a large pot. Add the lentils, the medium onion, garlic, bay leaf, and 1 teaspoon of the cumin. Return the soup to a boil and let it simmer for 30 minutes, or until the lentils are very soft. Let it cool slightly. Purée a quarter of the soup in a food processor or blender and return it to the pot.

2. Using the steel blade of the food processor, pulse the carrots, pepper, and the small onion until the vegetables are cut into ¼-inch slivers. (Do not process for so long that the vegetables are pureed.)

3. Reheat the soup and add the carrots, pepper, onion, vinegar, ginger, cinnamon, cayenne, and the additional 1 teaspoon cumin. Bring to a boil, reduce the heat to low, and simmer for 20 minutes, stirring occasionally to keep the soup from sticking.

8 SERVINGS
PER SERVING: 214 Calories • 0.8 Gram Fat • 3.2% Calories from Fat

Minestrone

This hearty soup can be easily doubled if you want to feed a crowd. Because it's made mostly of vegetables, you can afford a little bit of Parmesan cheese sprinkled on top for that authentic Italian taste.

5 cups water
2 garlic cloves, minced
2 teaspoons vegetable-broth mix
1 can (28 ounces) diced tomatoes
1 medium onion, chopped
2 stalks celery, chopped
2 cups cabbage, shredded
1 medium carrot, sliced
12 mushrooms, sliced
1 tablespoon chopped fresh basil
1 tablespoon chopped fresh oregano (or 1 teaspoon dried)
2 bay leaves
Salt and freshly ground black pepper
1 cup elbow macaroni, uncooked
2 tablespoons grated Parmesan cheese

1. In a large soup pot combine all the ingredients except the pasta and cheese and bring to a boil. Then reduce the heat and simmer for 1 hour. Add salt and pepper to taste.

2. Return the soup to a rolling boil and add the macaroni. Bring to a boil again and simmer until the pasta is cooked.

3. Serve in deep soup bowls and sprinkle Parmesan cheese, and additional pepper if you wish, on top.

6 SERVINGS
PER SERVING: 134 Calories • 1.5 Grams Fat • 9.7% Calories from Fat

Mushroom Barley Soup

This soup is a dense, satisfying food, nourishing, comforting, and warm—just what you need on a blustery cold winter night.

4 cups water
2 pounds onions, chopped
4 garlic cloves, minced
½ cup barley

¾ pound mushrooms, sliced
⅓ cup fresh parsley
2 teaspoons dried thyme
1 teaspoon low-sodium soy sauce

1. Place all the ingredients in a large soup pot and bring to a boil. Reduce the heat and simmer for 40 minutes. Let cool slightly.

2. Remove 2 cups of the soup and puree until smooth. (Puree only part so that some texture remains.) Return the puree to the soup. Reheat and add soy sauce to taste.

4 SERVINGS
PER SERVING: 165 Calories • 1.3 Grams Fat • 6.8% Calories from Fat

Parsnip Potato Soup

This midwinter soup will satisfy when you long for something creamy and soothing. And when the main ingredients are so very virtuous, you can add some Parmesan cheese. Try this with a Roasted Vegetable Hero (see page 117)

1 pound potatoes
1 pound parsnips
1 medium onion
3 cups nonfat chicken broth
3 garlic cloves

Salt
½ cup chopped fresh parsley
Freshly ground black pepper
2 tablespoons grated Parmesan cheese

1. Scrub the potatoes and cut into chunks. Scrape the parsnips and cut into chunks. Cut the onion into chunks.

2. In a soup pot, combine the broth and the potatoes, parsnips, onion, and garlic. Bring to a boil. Reduce the heat and simmer for 20 minutes, or until the vegetables are soft.

3. Let the soup cool slightly. In batches, puree the soup in a food processor or blender. Adjust with salt to taste. Return the soup to the pot and reheat. Serve with parsley, pepper to taste, and Parmesan sprinkled on top.

4 SERVINGS
PER SERVING: 175 Calories • 1.2 Grams Fat • 6.1% Calories from Fat

Manhattan Clam Chowder

This dinner soup can be on the table thirty minutes after you arrive home. Accompanied by a good hunk of bread and a small salad, it makes a meal that will leave you feeling whole and restored. Old Bay Seasoning is a widely used seasoning powder generally available at fish markets.

1 can (28 ounces) tomatoes, with juice
1 medium onion
1 medium potato
⅓ cup white wine
16 ounces bottled clam juice
1 bay leaf
1 can (13 ounces) clams, with liquid
½ teaspoon Old Bay Seasoning
1 tablespoon chopped fresh parsley

1. Retaining the juice from the can, dice the tomatoes into ½-inch pieces. Chop the onion, and cut the potato into ½-inch cubes.

2. Combine the tomatoes and the retained juice in a saucepan with the onion, potato, wine, clam juice, and bay leaf and bring to a boil. Reduce the heat and simmer for 15 minutes, or until the potato chunks are tender.

3. Retaining the liquid from the can, mince the clams. Add the clams, the retained liquid, and the seasoning to the ingredients in the saucepan and heat through. Serve hot with parsley sprinkled on top.

4 SERVINGS
PER SERVING: 132 Calories • 0.7 Gram Fat • 4.9% Calories from Fat

New England Clam Chowder

Clam-chowder fans come in two varieties: those who love the New England kind and those who prefer the Manhattan type. I have lived in both places, have friends in both places, and am loathe to alienate anybody, so I offer both.

1 medium onion, chopped
2 stalks celery, chopped
1 cup skim milk
2 tablespoons all-purpose flour
$\frac{1}{4}$ teaspoon salt

$\frac{3}{4}$ teaspoon minced fresh thyme
(or $\frac{1}{4}$ teaspoon dried)
1 medium potato, cooked and diced
1 can (12 ounces) clams, minced
Freshly ground black pepper

1. Coat a large nonstick skillet with cooking spray. Heat the pan over medium heat for 10 seconds and add the onions and celery. Brown for 4 minutes, or until the onion is soft and transparent. Remove and set aside.

2. In a food processor or blender, combine the milk, clam juice, flour, salt, and thyme. Heat the nonstick skillet for 30 seconds. Blend the milk mixture and pour into the hot pan. Stirring constantly, bring the milk mixture to a boil. Then let it simmer for 5 minutes.

3. Add the onions and celery, the diced potato, and the clams and their juice and heat through. Serve piping hot with freshly ground pepper to taste.

4 SERVINGS
PER SERVING: 90 Calories • 0.3 Gram Fat • 3.0% Calories from Fat

Borscht

This Russian favorite shows off the intense deep color of beets. Stirring in the yogurt cheese slowly will create the most luscious hues of pink in swirling patterns.

$\frac{3}{4}$ pound beets
$\frac{1}{2}$ medium onion
4 cups water
2 tablespoons apple-cider vinegar
1 tablespoon honey
2 tablespoons low-sodium soy sauce
2 teaspoons broth mix

$\frac{1}{2}$ cup tomato puree
1 tablespoon minced fresh dill
(or $\frac{1}{4}$ teaspoon dried)
plus extra dill for garnish
$1\frac{1}{2}$ cups nonfat plain yogurt cheese
(page 8)

1. Scrub the beets and cut them into chunks no larger than 2 inches per side. Quarter the onion. Place beets and onion in a medium-size saucepan with the water, vinegar, honey, soy sauce, broth mix, tomato puree, and dill. Simmer for 40 minutes, or until a knife can easily pierce through a chunk.

2. Let the soup cool a bit and then process, in batches, in a food processor with a steel blade or a blender. Return to the saucepan and heat. Serve with a dollop of yogurt cheese and, if you wish, a sprinkle of dill.

4 SERVINGS
PER SERVING: 118 Calories • 0.3 Gram Fat • 2.3% Calories from Fat

Iced Cucumber Soup

When you are too hot to cook, make this soup: This cool, refreshing dish takes about 5 minutes to prepare, and not a single appliance in your kitchen needs to heat up.

2 medium cucumbers, peeled
$1\frac{1}{2}$ cups nonfat plain yogurt
1 scallion, minced

$\frac{1}{4}$ cup snipped fresh dill
$\frac{1}{4}$ cup chopped fresh parsley
Salt and freshly ground black pepper

1. Set aside one half of a cucumber. Cut the remaining 1½ cucumbers into chunks. Place them in a food processor or blender and add the yogurt, half the scallion, the dill, and the parsley. Blend until smooth and pour it into a serving bowl.

2. Finely chop the remaining cucumber. Sprinkle it and the reserved scallion over the soup. Add salt and pepper to taste. Chill the soup if desired or serve immediately.

4 SERVINGS
PER SERVING: 77 Calories • 0.5 Gram Fat • 5.7% Calories from Fat

Carrot Papaya Soup

You will smile when you taste the unexpected sweetness of the papaya and the coolness of the yogurt.

2 cups carrots cut into 1-inch chunks
½ cup chopped onions
2½ cups nonfat vegetable broth
1 teaspoon grated fresh ginger

2 tablespoons frozen orange-juice concentrate
1 papaya
¾ cup nonfat vanilla yogurt

1. In a large saucepan, bring the carrots, onions, broth, ginger, and orange-juice concentrate to a boil. Reduce the heat and simmer for 15 minutes, or until the carrots are very soft. Remove the pot from the heat and let the soup cool.
2. Pour the soup into a food processor or blender and process until smooth. Return the soup to the saucepan and reheat.
3. Cut the papaya in half and remove the seeds. Scoop out the flesh and dice.
4. Ladle the soup into individual serving bowls. Drop in a dollop of yogurt and swirl with a spoon to create a pleasing pattern. Top with papaya in the center and serve.

4 SERVINGS
PER SERVING: 131 Calories • 0.4 Gram Fat • 2.6% Calories from Fat

Cold Tomato Soup with Shrimp

Do not attempt this soup with midwinter tomatoes, which have the consistency and taste of tennis balls. Only the ripest of midsummer tomatoes will do.

4 ripe tomatoes
1 cup nonfat yogurt
2 scallions

1 tablespoon lemon juice
4 large shrimp, cooked
16 snow peas

1. Bring a large saucepan of water to a boil. Drop in the tomatoes and let them boil for 1 minute. Then plunge them into ice-cold water; the skins should burst. When they have cooled slightly, remove the tomatoes and slip off the skins.
2. Combine the yogurt, tomatoes, one of the scallions, and the lemon juice in a blender and process until smooth. Pour the mixture into a serving bowl.
3. Cut each shrimp into 3 or 4 pieces. Cut the snow peas into 3 or 4 pieces on the diagonal. Mince the second scallion.
4. Pour the soup into bowls. Top with minced scallion, snow peas, and shrimp.

4 SERVINGS
PER SERVING: 82 Calories • 0.8 Gram Fat • 8.0% Calories from Fat

Ginger Cantaloupe Soup

This cool refreshing soup is bound to perk up appetites even on the hottest day of the year! The ginger adds an unexpected zing to this smooth, peach-colored delight.

1 large cantaloupe
⅔ cup nonfat vanilla yogurt cheese (page 8)
1 teaspoon powdered sugar
2 teaspoons lemon juice
3 tablespoons crystallized ginger
4 mint sprigs

1. Cut the cantaloupe in half and remove the seeds. Halve the sections again and reserve one quarter of the melon. Scoop the flesh from the rind and place in a food processor or a blender. Add the vanilla yogurt cheese, sugar, lemon juice, and 2 tablespoons of the crystallized ginger. Process until smooth. Chill for 1 hour.

2. Cut the flesh off the remaining cantaloupe quarter. Dice and set aside. Finely mince the remaining 1 tablespoon of crystallized ginger.

3. Blend the soup one more time and pour into individual bowls. Sprinkle with the reserved cantaloupe and the ginger. Garnish each with a mint sprig and serve.

4 SERVINGS
PER SERVING: 89 Calories • 0.3 Gram Fat • 4.0% Calories from Fat

SALADS

When we think low fat, most of us think of salads, and a tossed green salad pops into mind. But the boundaries of what qualifies as a salad have expanded, and so have the possibilities for creating appetizing *and* low-fat varieties that can be enjoyed as lunch dishes or light suppers as well as the traditional dinner course.

Roasted Red Peppers with Tarragon

This delicately flavored, very low-calorie dish can also be used as an appetizer and is delicious on a sandwich. You may substitute other fresh herbs, but the slightly sweet flavor of tarragon goes particularly well with the mildness of the red pepper.

3 large sweet red peppers
2 teaspoons cider vinegar
1 teaspoon honey mustard
1 teaspoon minced fresh tarragon
Salt and freshly ground black pepper

1. Preheat the broiler or grill. Have a brown paper bag ready.

2. Place the red peppers 6 inches under the broiler for about 6 minutes, or until nicely charred. If you're using a grill, the procedure will be the same; adjust the distance to the heat source so that the peppers char but do not burn. Rotate the peppers to char each side. Use wooden spoons and care in turning the peppers because you don't want to pierce them when turning. The timing of this broiling procedure will depend on the size of the peppers, so you'll need to watch them constantly. When the entire pepper has been roasted, remove it from the broiler and place in a paper bag. Fold the bag closed and let it sit for 10 minutes, to cool off. The steam produced in the bag will help to loosen the skin.

3. Remove the peppers from the bag and peel off the blackened skin. The skin should slip off very easily in big sections. Cut out the stem, remove the seeds, and slice the peppers into strips.

4. In a medium mixing bowl, whisk the vinegar, mustard, and tarragon. Place the pepper strips in the dressing, combine gently, and let the flavors blend for 30 minutes. Season with salt and pepper to taste. Serve chilled or at room temperature.

4 SERVINGS
PER SERVING: 17 Calories • 0.2 Gram Fat • 9.7% Calories from Fat

Raw Carrot and Beet Salad

Just as eating raw carrots is a very different experience from eating cooked ones so too is the taste of raw beets totally unlike that of cooked beets. This raw salad is as beautiful to look at as it is delicious to eat.

2 medium beets
1 medium carrot
$\frac{1}{4}$ cup minced Vidalia onion

$\frac{1}{3}$ cup nonfat sour cream
1 teaspoon balsamic vinegar

1. Chop the greens off the beets and reserve for another use. Wash and peel the beets and scrape the carrot. Grate the beet and the carrot in a food processor or with a hand grater and place in a medium-size serving bowl.
2. In a separate small bowl, mix the onion, sour cream, and vinegar. Pour the dressing over the vegetables and mix lightly. Serve chilled or at room temperature.

4 SERVINGS
PER SERVING: 41 Calories • 0.1 Gram Fat • 2.1% Calories from Fat

Beets in Balsamic Vinegar

Generally, beets are not very assertive, but the tartness of the balsamic vinegar and Granny Smith apple helps to make this beautiful-looking vegetable come alive.

$1\frac{1}{2}$ pounds beets
1 large Granny Smith apple, chopped
$\frac{1}{4}$ cup minced Vidalia onion
3 tablespoons balsamic vinegar

$1\frac{1}{2}$ tablespoons minced fresh dill
(or 2 teaspoons dried)
$\frac{1}{4}$ teaspoon freshly ground
black pepper

1. Cut the green tops off the beets and scrub them thoroughly. Place them in a medium-size saucepan and cover with water. Bring to a boil, cover, and simmer for 30 minutes, or until the beets are soft when pierced. Run cold water over them and let cool slightly.
2. When the beets are cool enough to handle, gently rub the skins off. Chop the beets into ¼-inch cubes. Combine with the apple, onion, vinegar, dill, and pepper. Mix well. Let the salad cool to room temperature before serving, or chill in the refrigerator if preferred. Stir occasionally so the dressing is absorbed evenly.

6 SERVINGS
PER SERVING: 46 Calories • 0.2 Gram Fat • 3.1% Calories from Fat

Endive Salad

The endive is a very common vegetable in Holland, and variations of this salad regularly appear on the dinner table there. The bitterness of the endive, the sourness of the apple, the creaminess of the dressing, and the bite of the chili create a contrast that you'll enjoy and remember.

2 Belgian endives
1 Granny Smith apple, chopped
$\frac{1}{4}$ lemon
$\frac{1}{3}$ cup nonfat sour cream

1 teaspoon ketchup
1 teaspoon fresh lemon juice
1 pinch of chili powder
Salt and freshly ground black pepper

1. Remove 12 endive leaves and set aside. Chop the remaining endives and place in a medium bowl. Combine with the apple pieces. Squeeze the juice from the lemon over the endive and apple. Add water to cover, and chill for 1 hour.
2. In a separate small bowl, mix the sour cream, ketchup, lemon juice, chili powder, and salt and pepper to taste.
3. Drain the chopped endives and apples, return to the bowl, and pour the dressing over the mixture, blending well. Arrange 3 endive leaves on each plate and place a serving of salad in the center.

4 SERVINGS
PER SERVING: 76 Calories • 0.5 Gram Fat • 5.5% Calories from Fat

Greens with Tomato-Herb Dressing

This dressing should be served cold. You can substitute herbs freely—especially in the summer, just use whatever you have in the garden.

2 scallions, cut in quarters
1 cup tomato puree
1 tablespoon balsamic vinegar
$\frac{1}{4}$ cup nonfat sour cream

$\frac{1}{4}$ cup chopped fresh parsley
2 tablespoons chopped fresh basil
Salt and freshly ground black pepper
6 cups mixed greens

1. Place the scallions, tomato puree, vinegar, sour cream, parsley, and basil in a food processor or blender and process until the herbs are reduced to tiny flecks.
2. Add salt and pepper to taste. Pour immediately over greens, toss, and serve.

4 SERVINGS
PER SERVING: 76 Calories • 0.4 Gram Fat • 4.5% Calories from Fat

Dilled Cucumber Salad

I made this for a Passover meal where one of the guests, not liking cucumbers, took only a polite helping. But because this simple salad brings out the crunchiest best of this modest vegetable, she took seconds.

1 large cucumber
1½ tablespoons apple-cider vinegar
¾ teaspoon honey
4 sprigs fresh dill plus 1 teaspoon minced

1. If the cucumber is waxed, peel it. If not, you may leave the peel on.
2. Slice the cucumber thinly, using either the thin slicer in a food processor or the slicer side of a hand grater. Place the cucumber slices in a bowl.
3. In a small mixing bowl, combine the vinegar, honey, and minced dill.
4. Pour the dressing over the cucumbers, mix well, and chill for 1 hour before serving. Decorate with sprigs of dill.

4 SERVINGS
PER SERVING: 23 Calories • 0.2 Gram Fat • 7.9% Calories from Fat

Asparagus in Balsamic Dijon Sauce

This dish can star as a salad or a light lunch. The baguette is a wonderful accompaniment to the sharp vinaigrette.

¾ pound asparagus
½ cup water
½ teaspoon vegetable-broth mix
1 tablespoon coarse prepared mustard

2 teaspoons balsamic vinegar
¼ teaspoon powdered ginger
1 baguette

1. Preheat the oven to 350°F.
2. Snap off the woody ends of the asparagus. Combine the water and broth mix in a skillet and add the asparagus. Steam until bright green and tender. Steaming time will depend on the thickness of the asparagus.
3. In a separate bowl, combine the mustard, vinegar, and ginger. Arrange the asparagus on a serving plate and pour the sauce over it.
4. Warm the baguette in the oven for 5 minutes. Slice and serve in a basket.

4 SERVINGS
PER SERVING: 327 Calories • 3.8 Grams Fat • 10.0% Calories from Fat

Broccoli Salad with Mustard Dressing

Broccoli is widely praised for its excellent nutritional benefits, and its pretty face has even been the inspiration for jewelry design. Its beautiful, bright-green color will be lost, though, if you overcook it.

4 cups broccoli florets
1 tablespoon balsamic vinegar
1 tablespoon Dijon mustard
1 shallot, minced
1 tablespoon nonfat sour cream

1. Use a steamer basket to steam the broccoli florets until bright green and crisp-tender. Run them briefly under cold water to stop the cooking process, then set aside.

2. In a small mixing bowl, whisk together the vinegar, mustard, shallots, and sour cream. Pour over the broccoli and mix well. Serve at room temperature, or chill and serve cold.

4 SERVINGS
PER SERVING: 56 Calories • 0.7 Gram Fat • 9.2% Calories from Fat

Corn Celery Basil Salad

In the summer you'll be looking for something to do with all that corn and basil, and this salad is a fresh idea.

$\frac{1}{2}$ cup nonfat mayonnaise
$\frac{1}{4}$ cup minced fresh basil
1 cup cooked corn kernels, fresh or frozen
vinegar
2 cups chopped celery
1 cup chopped red pepper
$\frac{1}{4}$ cup chopped Vidalia onion
Salt and freshly ground black pepper

1. In a mixing bowl combine the mayonnaise, basil, and vinegar. Add the corn, celery, red pepper, and onion and mix well. Chill for 1 hour. Add salt and pepper to taste before serving.

4 SERVINGS
PER SERVING: 74 Calories • 0.5 Gram Fat • 5.2% Calories from Fat

Kohlrabi Slaw

Kohlrabi has a radishlike bite, and the mint gives this variation on the usual slaw yet another refreshing taste.

8 ounces kohlrabi slices
2 medium carrots
1 scallion, minced
1 tablespoon nonfat mayonnaise
1 teaspoon lemon juice
1½ teaspoons minced fresh mint or ½ teaspoon dried

1. Peel the kohlrabi and the carrots. Using the shredding disc in a food processor, shred the kohlrabi and carrots. In a medium bowl mix them and the scallion together.

2. Mix the mayonnaise and lemon juice in a small bowl. Pour the dressing over the vegetables and toss well. Sprinkle mint leaves over all and serve cold.

4 SERVINGS
PER SERVING: 27 Calories • 0.1 Gram Fat • 3.3% Calories from Fat

Dijon Potato Salad

Potato salad is a must in the summertime. It's a perfect complement to BBQ Chicken or Lemon Chicken (see pages 74 and 85).

4 medium potatoes cut into 1-inch cubes
2 tablespoons water
½ small onion, chopped
⅓ cup nonfat plain yogurt
⅓ cup nonfat mayonnaise

4 basil leaves, minced
½ teaspoon Dijon mustard
1 teaspoon apple-cider vinegar
Salt and freshly ground black pepper

1. Boil the potatoes until tender. Add the water to a skillet and bring to a boil. Add the chopped onion, reduce the heat, and simmer until the onion is transparent.

2. In a large bowl whisk together the yogurt, mayonnaise, basil, mustard, and vinegar. Add the potato and onion and mix well. Add salt and pepper to taste.

4 SERVINGS
PER SERVING: 108 Calories • 0.3 Gram Fat • 2.7% Calories from Fat

Tomatoes Stuffed with Herbed Lentils

Tomatoes and lentils star in this colorful dish. The tomatoes must be large and ripe, and while uncooked lentils are specified, any leftover lentil salad will do just fine. You may also substitute chopped parsley or basil if cilantro isn't available.

$\frac{1}{2}$ cup lentils, uncooked
1 cup water
1 small onion minced
1 bay leaf
1$\frac{1}{2}$ teaspoons minced fresh thyme (or $\frac{1}{2}$ teaspoon dried)
$\frac{1}{4}$ teaspoon paprika
$\frac{1}{4}$ teaspoon salt
4 large tomatoes
2 tablespoons minced fresh cilantro

1. In a small saucepan, combine the lentils, water, onion, bay leaf, thyme, paprika, and salt. Bring to boil, reduce the heat, and simmer uncovered for 20 minutes, or until the lentils are soft.

2. Pour the lentils into a colander and let them drain for 10 minutes.

3. Meanwhile, cut the tops off the tomatoes and, with a melon baller or small spoon, scoop out the seeds and membranes, leaving the shells of the tomatoes intact. Drain the tomatoes upside down for 30 minutes.

4. When the lentils are drained and cool, fill the tomato shells. Top with the cilantro.

4 SERVINGS
PER SERVING: 116 Calories • 0.7 Gram Fat • 5.4% Calories from Fat

Three-Bean Salad with Balsamic Tarragon Dressing

Most bean salads are too heavy for my liking. In this one, though, the fresh cucumber and tomato lighten things up a bit.

1 cup frozen green beans
1 can (8 ounces) kidney beans, drained
1 can (8 ounces) garbanzo beans, drained
1 cup chopped fresh tomato ($\frac{2}{3}$ pound)
1 cup chopped cucumber
$1\frac{1}{2}$ tablespoons minced red onion
$\frac{1}{4}$ cup balsamic vinegar
$\frac{3}{4}$ teaspoon fresh minced tarragon (or $\frac{1}{4}$ teaspoon dried)

1. Cook the frozen green beans, drain, and cool. Combine the drained kidney and garbanzo beans, green beans, tomatoes, cucumber, and onion in a large bowl.

2. In a small bowl, combine the vinegar and tarragon. Add the vegetables, mix, and chill for 1 hour. Mix again before serving.

4 SERVINGS
PER SERVING: 138 Calories • 1.1 Grams Fat • 6.5% Calories from Fat

Adzuki, Grapefruit, and Scallion Salad

Adzuki beans are small, round, red beans with a very mild taste. Use any standard method to cook them, preferably after soaking them overnight.

2 cups Adzuki beans, cooked and drained
1 large grapefruit
$\frac{1}{4}$ cup chopped scallion
$\frac{1}{4}$ cup yogurt cheese (page 8)

$\frac{1}{4}$ cup fresh parsley
$\frac{1}{2}$ teaspoon brown sugar
Salt

1. Drain the Adzuki beans well. Peel and section the grapefruit. Chop the sections into 5 pieces and let them drain.

2. In a food processor or blender process the yogurt cheese, parsley, and brown sugar until the parsley pieces are very small.

3. Lightly toss the yogurt-cheese mixture with the beans, grapefruit, and scallion. Add salt to taste.

6 SERVINGS
PER SERVING: 244 Calories • 0.8 Gram Fat • 2.9% Calories from Fat

Granny Smith Coleslaw

The fresh, tart taste of the Granny Smith gives a great lift to this coleslaw.

$\frac{1}{4}$–$\frac{1}{2}$ small head cabbage (2$\frac{1}{2}$ cups shredded)
1 Granny Smith apple
$\frac{1}{3}$ cup nonfat mayonnaise
$\frac{1}{4}$ cup apple-cider vinegar
1 tablespoon apple juice

1. To shred the cabbage, cut the head in quarters and remove the solid core. Lay the quarters on a cutting board and thinly slice until you have 2½ cups to create finely shredded cabbage.

2. Peel and core the apple. Grate.

3. Whisk the mayonnaise, vinegar, and apple juice in a small mixing bowl. In a serving bowl, combine the cabbage and apple. Pour the dressing over, mix well, and serve cold.

6 SERVINGS
PER SERVING: 29 Calories • 0.1 Gram Fat • 1.9% Calories from Fat

Pear Radish Salad

The delight of this salad is in the contrast of the sweet, aromatic pear and the crunchy, sharp radish, so make sure those ingredients are at the peak of flavor.

2 tablespoons nonfat lemon yogurt
1 tablespoon lemon juice
$\frac{1}{2}$ teaspoon ground cardamom
1 large pear, diced
6 medium radishes minced

1. In a bowl combine the yogurt, lemon juice, and cardamom. Add the pear and radish and mix well. Chill until served.

4 SERVINGS
PER SERVING: 32 Calories • 0.2 Gram Fat • 5.4% Calories from Fat

Orange and Vidalia Salad with Balsamic Vinegar

This salad will wake up your mouth with flavor: sweet, sour, and sharp all at once. It is best served with foods that are not as assertive in flavor.

4 oranges
½ Vidalia onion
3 fresh basil leaves
2 cups fresh spinach leaves
2 tablespoons balsamic vinegar
Freshly ground black pepper

1. Peel the oranges and remove most of the white pith. Slice the oranges and remove the seeds. Slice the onion very thinly, keeping the slices intact. Make a chiffonade of the basil leaves by rolling them up and slicing the rolls. You'll end up with thin strips.

2. On individual serving plates arrange the spinach around the edge. Then alternate the orange and onion slices. Drizzle balsamic vinegar over all. Grind some pepper on the oranges and onions. Sprinkle on the basil strips. Serve cold.

4 SERVINGS
PER SERVING: 61 Calories • 0.5 Gram Fat • 4.3% Calories from Fat

Fruited Wheatberry Salad

Wheatberries have a delightful nutty crunch that makes them an instant favorite even with picky eaters. You can vary the fruits in this salad, depending on what you have on hand, but keep in mind that a single dried fruit will provide the necessary sweetness.

1 cup wheatberries
1 medium apple, chopped
$\frac{1}{4}$ cup currants
$\frac{2}{3}$ cup mandarin orange sections
$\frac{1}{2}$ cup lowfat vanilla yogurt cheese (page 8)
$\frac{1}{2}$ teaspoon ground cinnamon
18 endive leaves

1. Bring 3 cups of water to a boil and add the wheatberries. Cook, covered, for 2 hours, or until soft. Drain if necessary and cool.

2. Place the apple pieces, currants, orange sections, yogurt cheese, and cinnamon in a bowl and mix well. Add the wheatberries and mix again.

3. Arrange 4 endive leaves around each serving plate and place the salad in the center, slightly overlapping the leaves. Serve cold.

6 SERVINGS
PER SERVING: 371 Calories • 3.4 Grams Fat • 7.3% Calories from Fat

Wheatberry Herb Salad

Wheatberry salad is one of my favorite lunches to take hiking: Its crunchy bite satisfies as no pasta does, and I can vary the vegetables in this salad to include what I have on hand. Try this salad sometimes with tomatoes and fresh basil, or carrots and fresh dill.

1 cup wheatberries
1 medium sweet red pepper, minced
2 scallions, minced
1 cup cucumbers, diced
$\frac{1}{3}$ cup minced fresh parsley
1 tablespoon minced fresh mint
$\frac{1}{3}$ cup nonfat mayonnaise
2 teaspoons lemon juice
Salt and freshly ground black pepper

1. Bring 3 cups of water to a boil and add the wheatberries. Cover and simmer for 2 hours, or until the wheatberries are soft. Cool.

2. In a mixing bowl, combine the cooked wheatberries, red pepper, scallions, cucumbers, parsley, mint, mayonnaise, and lemon juice. Add salt and pepper to taste. Mix well and refrigerate for 1 hour. Serve cold.

6 SERVINGS
PER SERVING: 110 Calories • 0.5 Gram Fat • 4.0% Calories from Fat

Quinoa Cilantro Salad Sandwiches

This sweet little grain is gaining popularity and can easily be used in place of rice. It's a whole grain that cooks up very quickly, and, for a grain, it supplies generous amounts of protein. If you haven't yet given it a whirl, try it in this delightful salad.

1 cup quinoa
2 cups water
1 tablespoon fresh minced mint (or 1 teaspoon dried)
$\frac{3}{4}$ teaspoon ground cumin
$\frac{1}{2}$ teaspoon ground coriander
$\frac{1}{2}$ teaspoon salt
1$\frac{1}{2}$ cups chopped tomato (about 1 pound)
1$\frac{1}{2}$ cups chopped cucumbers (1–2 whole)
$\frac{1}{4}$ cup minced fresh cilantro
1 tablespoon balsamic vinegar
4 pita breads
Salt and freshly ground black pepper

1. Place the quinoa in a strainer and run cold water over it for 30 seconds. Let it drain slightly and then place the quinoa in a medium-size saucepan. Add the water, mint, cumin, coriander, and salt. Bring to a boil, stir, cover, and reduce the heat. Let simmer for 25 minutes, or until all the water is absorbed. The grain is done when it looks translucent and has a visible little (germ) ring. Remove the pot from the heat and let the quinoa cool.

2. Meanwhile, combine the tomatoes, cucumbers, cilantro, and vinegar in a medium-size mixing bowl.

3. When the quinoa is cool, mix it well with the tomato-and-cucumber mixture. Let the salad chill, covered, in the refrigerator for 1 hour. Add salt, pepper, and possibly a little more balsamic vinegar to taste. Cut each pita bread into wedges and arrange in a circle around each serving plate. Spoon the salad into the middle.

4 SERVINGS
PER SERVING: 347 Calories • 3.6 Grams Fat • 9.2% Calories from Fat

Upper West Side Pasta Salad

I first made this salad during the late '70s, while I was living on the Upper West Side of Manhattan, busily tending my firstborn. It can easily be adapted to what you have on hand. Try cilantro instead of the parsley, or pine nuts for walnuts, for example.

Pasta ingredients

8 ounces shell pasta

1 ounce chopped walnuts

1 tomato, chopped

1 scallion, minced

4 black olives, sliced

$\frac{1}{4}$ cup minced fresh parsley

Dressing ingredients

2 tablespoons nonfat sour cream

1 tablespoon balsamic vinegar

1 teaspoon Dijon mustard

1 teaspoon grated Parmesan cheese

1. Cook the pasta, following the package directions, until al dente. Rinse under cold water to stop the cooking process and drain.

2. In a large bowl combine the walnuts, tomato, scallion, olives, and parsley. Mix well. Add the cooled pasta and stir completely.

3. In a small bowl, thoroughly combine the sour cream, vinegar, and mustard.

4. Just before serving, pour the dressing over the salad, mix well, and sprinkle the cheese on the top.

4 SERVINGS
PER SERVING: 245 Calories • 2.6 Grams Fat • 9.8% Calories from Fat

Honey-Mustard Dressing

This is a strong-flavored dressing, and it tastes best on strong-flavored greens, such as arugula and watercress.

$\frac{1}{4}$ cup apple-cider vinegar
1 tablespoon honey mustard
1 tablespoon honey
1 tablespoon nonfat sour cream

1. Stir all the ingredients until the mixture is smooth. Refrigerate.
2. Mix again right before serving.

1 RECIPE—4 SERVINGS
PER SERVING: 102 Calories • 1.2 Grams Fat • 9.6% Calories from Fat

Creamy Mustard Dressing

Making good salad dressings, especially creamy ones, is one of the greatest challenges when you're watching your fat intake. Fat-free mayonnaise, yogurt, and sour cream are your best friends in this department. I find other fat-free dairy products to be sub-standard, and I don't use them. The industry keeps improving the quality of these products, however, so who knows what might be available in the future.

$\frac{1}{3}$ cup nonfat mayonnaise
3 tablespoons apple juice
1 tablespoon Dijon mustard
1 tablespoon finely minced shallot
1 tablespoon balsamic vinegar
1 teaspoon light miso
$\frac{1}{4}$ teaspoon freshly ground black pepper
$\frac{3}{4}$ teaspoon minced fresh oregano (or $\frac{1}{4}$ teaspoon dried)
Salt

1. Combine the mayonnaise, apple juice, mustard, shallot, vinegar, miso, pepper, and oregano. Let the flavors blend for 1 hour.
2. Add salt to taste and toss with your favorite green salad.

1 RECIPE—4 SERVINGS
PER SERVING: 120 Calories • 1.1 Grams Fat • 8.1% Calories from Fat

BREADS

Most breads easily qualify for the 10-percent-of-calories-from-fat classification. Their high complex-carbohydrate content offsets whatever fat is used in their preparation. Stay away from the majority of commercial muffins, though, for their fat content can well exceed the limit. Try bagels instead, or whole-grain breads, but avoid the butter or cream cheese that many people slather on. In their place try jelly and apple butter, which taste great and don't contribute a single fat gram to your daily intake.

Biscuits

Ordinarily biscuits are chock-full of fat calories, but these are ever so virtuous. They're fast and easy, too, so you can treat yourself and your family to these frequently. Don't spoil the whole idea by heaping the biscuits with high-fat toppings: Use a yogurt cheese (see page 8) or jelly instead.

1 cup and 3 tablespoons all-purpose flour
1 cup whole-wheat flour
2 tablespoons sugar
1 tablespoon oat bran
$1\frac{1}{2}$ teaspoons baking soda
$\frac{1}{2}$ teaspoon salt
1 cup plus 1 tablespoon buttermilk

1. Preheat the oven to 350°F.

2. In a large mixing bowl, combine the flours, sugar, oat bran, baking soda, and salt. Add the 1 cup of buttermilk and stir with a wooden spoon until the flour comes together. If necessary, use your hands to mix.

3. Turn the dough out onto a floured board and knead for 15 seconds. With the palms of your hands, flatten the dough until it's ½-inch to ¾-inch thick. Using a small glass as a biscuit form, punch out circles of dough and place them on an ungreased baking sheet. Reform the remaining dough and repeat the process until all has been used. Try not to handle the dough too much. Brush the tops of the biscuits with the additional buttermilk.

4. Bake the biscuits for 15 minutes, or until done.

8 SERVINGS
PER SERVING: 135 Calories • 0.8 Gram Fat • 5.0% Calories from Fat

Cinnamon Muffins

These muffins will make the whole kitchen smell heavenly. Serve them with a sweet yogurt cheese (see page 8) or nonfat cream cheese.

½ cup skim milk
¼ cup nonfat vanilla yogurt
1 cup unsweetened applesauce
¼ cup brown sugar
½ teaspoon vinegar
¼ teaspoon salt
1 cup all-purpose flour
1 cup whole-wheat flour
1 teaspoon baking soda
1 teaspoon ground cinnamon
½ teaspoon ground cloves
½ teaspoon ground allspice

1. Preheat the oven to 375°F. Coat a 12-cup muffin tin with cooking spray. (Don't use paper baking cups.)

2. In a medium-size mixing bowl, whisk together the milk, yogurt, applesauce, sugar, and vinegar.

3. Sift into another bowl the salt, flour, baking soda, cinnamon, cloves, and allspice.

4. Combine the flour mixture with the applesauce mixture lightly, until the flour is just wet. Spoon into the cups of the muffin tin and bake for 20 minutes, or until done. Remove from tin and serve immediately.

12 SERVINGS
PER SERVING: 105 Calories • 0.3 Gram Fat • 2.3% Calories from Fat

Pumpkin Muffins

These yummy and chewy muffins are not too sweet and have almost a full day's supply of vitamin A.

$\frac{1}{2}$ cup skim milk

$\frac{1}{4}$ cup nonfat yogurt

1 cup canned pumpkin

$\frac{1}{2}$ cup brown sugar

$\frac{1}{2}$ cup unsweetened applesauce

$\frac{1}{2}$ teaspoon apple-cider vinegar

$\frac{1}{4}$ teaspoon salt

2 cups all-purpose flour

$\frac{1}{2}$ teaspoon baking powder

1 teaspoon baking soda

$1\frac{1}{2}$ teaspoons cinnamon

1 teaspoon allspice

$\frac{1}{2}$ teaspoon ground cloves

1. Preheat the oven to 375°F. Coat a 12-cup muffin tin with cooking spray. (Don't use paper baking cups.)

2. In a large mixing bowl, combine the milk, yogurt, pumpkin, sugar, applesauce, vinegar, and salt. Mix well.

3. Sift together the flour, baking powder, baking soda, cinnamon, allspice, and cloves in a separate large mixing bowl.

4. Add the flour mixture in 3 batches to the pumpkin mixture until all is well mixed. Spoon the dough into the cups of the muffin tin and bake for 40 minutes, or until done. Serve hot.

12 SERVINGS
PER SERVING: 118 Calories • 0.3 Gram Fat • 2.5% Calories from Fat

Dill Parmesan Scones

These scones are so simple to make and so delicious. If you want to have them often, make the flour mixture in advance and store it in self-sealing plastic bags.

$1\frac{1}{4}$ cups all-purpose flour
2 teaspoons pasteurized dried egg whites
1 teaspoon baking powder
$\frac{1}{4}$ teaspoon baking soda
$\frac{1}{4}$ teaspoon salt
$\frac{3}{4}$ teaspoon minced fresh dill or $\frac{1}{4}$ teaspoon dried
1 tablespoon plus 1 teaspoon grated Parmesan cheese
$\frac{3}{4}$ cup nonfat plain yogurt

1. Preheat the oven to 425°F. Coat a nonstick baking sheet with cooking spray.

2. Sift the flour, pasteurized dried egg whites, baking powder, baking soda, salt, and dill into a mixing bowl. Mix in the tablespoon of Parmesan cheese. Add the yogurt and stir until the mixture is doughy. Form the dough into a ball and place it on the baking sheet.

3. Flatten out the ball slightly and cut the dough into six wedges by making three long crosscuts. Separate the triangular scones. Sprinkle the remaining Parmesan on top.

4. Bake the scones for 12 minutes, or until they're slightly brown.

6 SERVINGS
PER SERVING: 119 Calories • 0.6 Gram Fat • 5.0% Calories from Fat

Ginger Scones

Ginger scones go equally well with a hot cup of tea or a hot bowl of soup. Try them with the Acorn Squash Tomato Soup (page 16). If you like, you can replace the ginger with the more traditional currants: Add ¼ cup of currants to the flour mixture before adding the yogurt.

$1\frac{1}{4}$ cups all-purpose flour (reserve 1 tablespoon)
1 tablespoon sugar
2 teaspoons pasteurized dried egg whites
1 teaspoon baking powder
$\frac{1}{4}$ teaspoon baking soda
$\frac{1}{4}$ teaspoon salt
$\frac{3}{4}$ cup nonfat vanilla yogurt
1 tablespoon minced crystallized ginger

1. Preheat the oven to 425°F. Coat a nonstick baking sheet with cooking spray.
2. In a large mixing bowl, sift the flour, sugar, pasteurized dried egg white, baking powder, baking soda, and salt. Mix well.
3. In a small bowl, combine the vanilla yogurt and ginger.
4. Add the wet ingredients to the dry ingredients, and stir until just combined. Sprinkle the reserved tablespoon of flour on a work surface and turn out the dough. Flip it over once so flour will coat both sides. Lightly pat the dough into a 12-inch circle and cut the circle into 8 wedges. Transfer them with a spatula onto the prepared baking sheet.
5. Bake the scones for 12 to 15 minutes, or until golden brown.

8 SERVINGS
PER SERVING: 101 Calories • 0.2 Gram Fat • 2.1% Calories from Fat

Corny Dill Corn Bread

This very simple corn bread can be on the table in 30 minutes, and it's a perfect accompaniment to a bowl of soup.

1 cup cornmeal
$\frac{2}{3}$ cup all-purpose flour
1$\frac{1}{2}$ teaspoons baking powder
1 tablespoon snipped fresh dill (or 1 teaspoon dried)
$\frac{1}{2}$ teaspoon baking soda
$\frac{1}{2}$ teaspoon salt
2 egg whites (or 4 teaspoons pasteurized dried egg whites
plus $\frac{1}{4}$ cup water)
1 can (15$\frac{1}{4}$ ounces) corn, drained
1 cup nonfat plain yogurt

1. Preheat oven the oven to 400°F.

2. Coat a nonstick 9 by 9-inch pan with cooking spray. In a large bowl, combine the cornmeal, flour, baking powder, dill, baking soda, and salt.

3. In a smaller bowl, whip up the pasteurized dried egg whites until they're lightly foamy. Add the corn and yogurt and mix well. Add the wet ingredients to the dry ingredients and combine.

4. Pour the batter into the prepared pan and smooth out the top. Bake for 20 to 25 minutes, or until a toothpick inserted in the middle comes out clean and dry.

9 SERVINGS
PER SERVING: 211 Calories • 2.2 Grams Fat • 8.6% Calories from Fat

Soda Bread

This loaf can be on the table minutes from the time you decide you want some warm bread. Usually Irish soda bread is made with whole caraway seeds, but I don't happen to like them, so this bread is without. If you choose to include them, add with the oat bran and omit the currants.

1 cup nonfat plain yogurt
2 tablespoons brown sugar
1 tablespoon water
$1\frac{1}{3}$ cups flour
1 teaspoon baking soda
$\frac{1}{4}$ teaspoon salt
$\frac{1}{4}$ cup oat bran
$\frac{1}{3}$ cup currants

1. Coat a nonstick baking sheet with cooking spray. Preheat the oven to 350°F.

2. In a large mixing bowl, combine the yogurt, brown sugar, and water. Stir well. Over this sift the flour, baking soda, and salt. Add the oat bran and currants and mix well but gently.

3. Turn the dough out onto a floured board and sprinkle a little flour over the top. Knead it 5 times and then shape into a flat ball. Place the ball of dough on the prepared baking sheet and with a very sharp knife make a ½-inch deep X on the top of the dough.

4. Bake for 30 minutes, or until nicely brown and a wooden skewer inserted in the center comes out clean.

4 SERVINGS
PER SERVING: 250 Calories • 1.0 Gram Fat • 3.5% Calories from Fat

Zucchini Parmesan Jalapeño Flat Bread

When you discover yet another beautiful zucchini in the garden and your family moans in dismay, make everyone happy and serve this great bread.

1 cup flour
1 teaspoon baking powder
½ teaspoon vegetable-broth mix
2 egg whites (or 4 teaspoons pasteurized dried egg whites plus ¼ cup water)
1 cup shredded zucchini
¼ cup nonfat plain yogurt
½ jalapeño pepper, minced
2 tablespoons grated Parmesan cheese

1. Preheat oven to 350°F. Coat a 9 by 9-inch nonstick baking pan with cooking spray.

2. In a large bowl, sift the flour, baking powder, and broth mix.

3. In a medium-size bowl beat the egg whites (or pasteurized dried egg whites) until frothy. Add the zucchini, yogurt, jalapeño, and Parmesan and blend well. Stir in the zucchini mixture with the flour mixture and combine well.

4. Spread the dough on the prepared pan and smooth over the top. Bake for 40 minutes, or until a skewer inserted in the center comes out clean.

6 SERVINGS
PER SERVING: 99 Calories • 0.8 Gram Fat • 6.9% Calories from Fat

ENTRÉES

Perhaps the most formidable challenge fat-conscious diners face is finding main dishes that are filling, nutritious, and delicious. Some have found that eliminating fat depletes their food of flavor altogether; others, over time, acquire a preference for truly low-fat foods. Whether you're just embarking on the 10-percent-or-less low-fat journey or you're a seasoned traveler, you should find favorites among the recipes that follow.

Traditional nonvegetarian choices for main-course dishes have been beef, pork, chicken, or fish. The strict requirements of a 10-percent-or-less diet prohibit using beef or pork because of their high fat content, even in the leanest cuts. Chicken and turkey, when cooked without their skins, do fit within the 10-percent criterion, provided the other ingredients used to prepare them also comply. Most fish is easy to adapt to strict low-fat diets, with the exception of certain "meatier" varieties, such as salmon and mackerel.

Vegetarian main dishes bypass the problem of avoiding high-fat meats and fish, but new challenges must be met. To obtain the necessary protein without the fat that so often accompanies them, use the various meat substitutes and soy foods that are increasingly available in supermarkets. With the wonderful array of fresh herbs, vegetables, and fruits in most supermarkets, vegetarian foods have gained a new status and attracted a whole new audience. They're a far cry from the old bland, fat-filled standbys.

In tandem with a new look at the ingredients we use in main dishes must be a reconsideration of the methods of preparing them. Different ways of sautéing, frying, and roasting replace the standard reliance on oil, butter, and other fats. Steaming, sautéing, and clay-pot roasting are naturals for low-fat cooking.

With imagination and a willingness to explore new culinary territories, you *can* have delicious low-fat main course that will satisfy almost every palate.

FISH

Denizens of the deep rise to the top when their fat grams are being compared with meats and poultry. With a few exceptions, such as salmon and mackerel, fish is low in fat yet high in flavor, making it the perfect food for low-fat diets. If you can't afford crab or lobster, substitute the inexpensive processed fish—usually pollack—called surimi. Its taste is not as deep as the real thing, but it approaches the original in texture.

Bouillabaisse

I discovered bouillabaisse in Paris when I was only fifteen and, consequently, too young to appreciate it. It apparently is best suited to adult taste; my children don't find it appetizing, either. Feel free to experiment with different combinations of firm, white fish fillets in addition to the cod.

1 medium onion, chopped	1 cup white wine
2 garlic cloves, minced	16 ounces bottled clam juice
2 stalks celery, chopped	Pinch of saffron
1 medium leek, chopped	$\frac{1}{2}$ pound cod fillets
1 fennel bulb, chopped	$\frac{1}{2}$ pound scallops
1 teaspoon dried thyme	$\frac{1}{2}$ pound shrimp
1 can (16 ounces) tomatoes, chopped	$\frac{1}{2}$ pound lobster

1. Coat a nonstick skillet with cooking spray and heat for 30 seconds. Add the onion and cook until it starts to turn color. Add the garlic and brown for 1 minute more. Place the mixture in a large soup pot.

2. Mix the celery, leek, fennel, and thyme into the skillet and sauté for a few minutes, stirring frequently. Add the leek mixture to the onions in the soup pot.

3. Add the tomatoes, wine, clam juice, and saffron to the soup pot and bring to a boil. Reduce the heat and simmer for 20 minutes.

4. Add the cod, scallops, shrimp, and lobster. Stir well. Simmer very gently for about 10 minutes, or until the fish is cooked through.

8 SERVINGS
PER SERVING: 174 Calories • 1.4 Grams Fat • 8.1% Calories from Fat

Clam Rice with Shrimp

This elegant and colorful one-pot meal can be on the table in half an hour if you hustle.

1 cup water
16 ounces bottled clam juice
½ medium onion, chopped
1 garlic clove, minced
2 stalks celery, chopped
8 ounces mushrooms, sliced
Salt
1 cup white rice
16 medium shrimp
2 cups frozen peas
¼ cup minced fresh parsley
4 tablespoons grated Parmesan cheese
Freshly ground black pepper

1. Bring the water and clam juice to a boil in a medium-size saucepan. Add the onion, garlic, celery, mushrooms, and salt to taste. Simmer for 10 minutes.

2. Add the rice and return to a boil. Reduce the heat, cover, and simmer for 15 minutes.

3. Meanwhile, clean the shrimp by removing the hard outer shell. With a sharp knife make a slit on the outside curve of the shrimp and, under running water, remove any black grit you might find. Do not cut all the way through the shrimp.

4. When the 15 minutes are up, add the frozen peas to the rice and mix. Salt to taste. Place the shrimp on top of the rice and cover. After 3 minutes turn the shrimp over and continue to heat through until they're pink and done. Sprinkle the parsley and Parmesan on top and add pepper to taste. Serve immediately.

4 SERVINGS
PER SERVING: 386 Calories • 3.5 Grams Fat • 8.2% Calories from Fat

Crab Rice Stuffed Peppers

Stuffed peppers can be sophisticated, as this crab-laced version proves. If you can find them, use purple bell peppers for an unusual visual effect.

4 medium sweet peppers
2 cups nonfat chicken broth
1 cup white rice
1 medium onion, minced

1½ teaspoons minced fresh thyme
or ½ teaspoon dried
9 ounces crabmeat
Salt and freshly ground black pepper

1. Put a large pot of water to boil and preheat the oven to 375°F.
2. Cut the tops off the peppers and remove the seeds and membranes. Take the pot of boiling water from the heat. Place the peppers in the hot water for 10 minutes. Remove them and let them drain upside down.
3. In a medium-size saucepan, bring the chicken broth to a boil. Add the rice and onion and return to a boil. Stir, cover, and simmer for 20 minutes, or until the rice is done. Add the crabmeat. Add salt and pepper to taste. Cool a little.
4. Pour ½ cup of water in an oven-proof dish. Fill the cavities of the peppers with the rice mixture and arrange in the dish. Cover and bake for 25 minutes, or until the rice is heated through and the peppers are soft.

4 SERVINGS
PER SERVING: 269 Calories • 1.3 Grams Fat • 4.4% Calories from Fat

Cod with Tomatoes and Dill

This is a simple and fresh way to present a good piece of fish. Add plain boiled potatoes to soak up the sauce.

3 tomatoes, sliced
2 scallions, green and white parts, sliced
1 pound cod
½ cup white wine

2 tablespoons minced fresh dill
(or 2 teaspoons dried)
Salt and freshly ground black pepper

1. Preheat the oven to 350°F. Place the tomatoes in a baking dish, sprinkle the scallions over them, and top with the fish fillets. Pour the wine over all, and sprinkle the dill on top. Cover with aluminum foil, crimping the edges.
2. Bake for 20 minutes, or until the fish is cooked. Add salt and pepper to taste.

4 SERVINGS
PER SERVING: 138 Calories • 1.1 Grams Fat • 8.6% Calories from Fat

Shrimp on a Bed of Vegetables

Serve this dish over a plain, dry rice so that you can enjoy the flavors of all the different vegetables.

2 stalks celery, chopped
½ cup sweet green pepper, chopped
½ cup sweet red pepper, chopped
½ cup crimini mushrooms, sliced
1 teaspoon minced scallion
1 garlic clove, minced
2 tomatoes, chopped
¼ cup white wine
½ teaspoon salt
1 teaspoon minced fresh basil
1 pound shrimp, cooked
Freshly ground black pepper

1. Coat a nonstick skillet with cooking spray. Heat for 20 seconds. Add the celery, peppers, mushrooms, scallion, garlic, and tomatoes, stirring constantly. Cook for 2 minutes. Add the wine, salt, and basil. Cook for 10 minutes.
2. Stir in the shrimp and heat through. Grind pepper over all before serving.

4 SERVINGS
PER SERVING: 147 Calories • 1.6 Grams Fat • 10.0% Calories from Fat

Shrimp Kabobs on Saffron Rice

Skewers of grilled vegetables and shrimp on beds of yellow saffron rice: This can hardly be called a "sacrifice" by any stretch of the imagination.

1 pound large shrimp
Juice of 1 lemon
$\frac{1}{4}$ cup white wine
1 teaspoon Dijon mustard
1 teaspoon minced shallot
$\frac{1}{2}$ teaspoon minced garlic
Dash hot sauce
2 cups water
1 cup white rice
$\frac{1}{2}$ teaspoon salt
$\frac{1}{8}$ teaspoon saffron
24 cherry tomatoes
1 medium sweet green pepper, cut in 1-inch chunks

1. Peel and devein the shrimp, leaving the tails on. In a large bowl, mix the lemon juice, wine, mustard, shallot, garlic, and hot sauce. Add the shrimp, cover the bowl, and refrigerate for at least 1 hour.

2. Soak wooden skewers in water for 20 minutes. Start the grill or preheat the broiler.

3. While the shrimp marinate, prepare the rice. Bring the water to a boil. Stir in the rice, salt, and saffron. Bring to a second boil and reduce the heat. Cover and simmer for 20 minutes, or until done.

4. Remove the shrimp from the marinade and skewer them, alternating with the tomatoes and peppers. (The best way to skewer the shrimp is to let them maintain their natural C shape and make the skewer go through twice, forming a D with the skewer.)

5. Broil or grill the shrimp for about 3 minutes on each side, or until they are cooked through. Fluff the rice with a fork. Serve with the shrimp, tomatoes, and peppers over it.

4 SERVINGS
PER SERVING: 322 Calories • 2.6 Grams Fat • 7.4% Calories from Fat

Paella

There are as many "authentic" paellas as there are "authentic" tomato sauces. Every cook has one. Use this recipe as a guideline, and experiment until you have your own authentic version.

1 medium onion, minced
3 cloves garlic, minced
1½ cups nonfat chicken broth
¾ cup white wine
Pinch of saffron
1 cup white rice
1 medium sweet green pepper, chopped
1 medium sweet red pepper, chopped
1 package (15 ounces) frozen artichoke hearts, quartered
1 cup peas
1 skinless chicken-breast half, cut in 1-inch cubes
6 large shrimp
1 pound clams
½ pound crabmeat

1. Preheat the oven to 375°F. Combine the onion, garlic, broth, wine, and saffron in a medium-size saucepan and bring to a boil. Add the rice and stir. Reduce the heat, cover, and let simmer for 20 minutes, or until the rice is done.

2. Add the peppers, artichoke hearts, peas, and chicken. Mix well. Let the ingredients heat through for 5 minutes on very low heat.

3. Clean the shrimp, leaving the tails on. Devein. Cut an incision in the last ¾ inch of the tails, along the deveining incision.

4. Scrub the clams clean. Place a steamer basket in a saucepan with water and bring to a boil. Steam the clams open in 5 to 10 minutes. Discard any that fail to open. Time it so that the clams will be done when the rice comes out of the oven.

5. Turn the rice out into an ovenproof casserole dish. Place the shrimp and crabmeat on top, pushing them slightly into the rice. Heat through for 5 minutes in the oven, or until the seafood is cooked. Turn the shrimp once to cook the other sides. Place clams on top and serve.

6 SERVINGS
PER SERVING: 211 Calories • 2.0 Grams Fat • 9.4% Calories from Fat

Fish Stew with Shells and Spinach

This nourishing one-pot meal can be made in 20 minutes, provides you with an astonishing supply of nutrients, and is delicious, besides. If you prefer, you may substitute another white fish fillet or crab for the sole.

1 pound sole fillet
1 cup chopped tomatoes
$\frac{1}{2}$ 10-ounce package (5 ounces) frozen chopped spinach
$\frac{1}{2}$ cup chopped sweet green pepper
1 cup clam juice
2 cups vegetable-juice cocktail
1 teaspoon dried thyme
2 tablespoons minced fresh basil
4 ounces pasta shells
2 tablespoons grated Parmesan cheese

1. Cut the sole into bite-size pieces and set aside.

2. In a large pot, combine the tomatoes, spinach, green pepper, clam juice, vegetable juice, thyme, and 1 tablespoon of the basil. Simmer for about 10 minutes.

3. Add the pasta shells and bring to a boil. Cook for 5 minutes.

4. Add the sole and reduce the heat. Simmer, stirring frequently, for 3 to 6 minutes, or until the fish and pasta are done. Serve in large bowls with the remaining basil and the Parmesan cheese sprinkled on top.

4 SERVINGS
PER SERVING: 266 Calories • 2.2 Grams Fat • 7.5% Calories from Fat

Mussels in Vermouth

If you buy farm-raised mussels, you won't have to scrub so much. Otherwise have your fishmonger show you how to clean them.

2 cups water
2 tablespoons minced onion
2 tablespoons minced celery
$\frac{1}{4}$ teaspoon salt

1 cup white rice
1 cup vermouth
4 garlic cloves
1 pound mussels, cleaned

1. Bring 2 cups of water to a boil in a medium-size saucepan. Add the onion, celery, and salt, and stir. Add the rice, and bring to a boil. Reduce the heat, cover, and simmer for 20 minutes, or until the rice is done.
2. Pour the vermouth and garlic into a medium-size saucepan and place the mussels over them. When the rice is almost done, bring the vermouth to a boil, cover the pot, and let the mussels steam for 5 minutes, or until they open. Discard any that don't open.
3. Serve the mussels with some of the broth over the hot rice.

4 SERVINGS
PER SERVING: 361 Calories • 2.9 Grams Fat • 9.3% Calories from Fat

Mustard Honey Scallops

This is a huge burst of taste—nothing boring or restrictive about this dish. Serve with mild-mannered Sweet Onion Basmati Rice (page 124).

$\frac{1}{4}$ cup honey
$\frac{1}{4}$ cup Dijon mustard
2 tablespoons orange juice, frozen concentrate
$\frac{1}{2}$ teaspoon grated ginger
$\frac{1}{4}$ teaspoon cumin powder

$\frac{1}{4}$ teaspoon curry powder
16 sea scallops, whole
$\frac{1}{4}$ teaspoon olive oil
1 cup watercress

1. In a medium-size bowl, mix the honey, mustard, orange juice, ginger, cumin, and curry. Spread the honey-mustard mixture over the scallops, and let them marinate for 30 minutes.
2. Rub the olive oil on a large skillet. Add the scallops and marinade and cook gently for 5 minutes; then turn the scallops over and cook for 3 minutes, or until done.
3. Serve the scallops on a bed of the watercress and pour the sauce over all.

4 SERVINGS
PER SERVING: 130 Calories • 1.3 Grams Fat • 8.8% Calories from Fat

ENTRÉES

Haddock with Three Citrus Salsa

This citrus salsa will perk up any number of dishes that need a fresh, bright accompaniment.

16 ounces haddock
Juice of 1 lime
Juice of 1 orange
1 teaspoon tamari soy sauce
1 orange
$\frac{1}{4}$ lemon
$\frac{1}{2}$ grapefruit
$\frac{1}{3}$ cup minced cucumber
1 tablespoon minced shallot
1 teaspoon minced fresh mint
1 teaspoon balsamic vinegar

1. Place the haddock in a shallow bowl. Combine the lime and orange juices with the soy sauce and pour over the haddock. Cover the bowl and let marinate in the refrigerator for at least 1 hour.

2. While the fish marinates, prepare the salsa. Peel the orange, lemon, and grapefruit. Remove the white pith. Loosen the sections, discarding the membranes. Cut each section into thirds.

3. Combine the citrus chunks with the cucumber, shallot, mint, and vinegar. Refrigerate until ready to serve.

4. Just before you're ready to eat, preheat the broiler and remove the haddock from the marinade. Broil the haddock until cooked through. (The length of time will depend on the thickness. Allow 7 to 8 minutes for 1 inch of thickness.) Serve with citrus salsa on the side.

4 SERVINGS
PER SERVING: 140 Calories • 1.0 Gram Fat • 6.0% Calories from Fat

Flounder Florentine

This is a classic and classy dish with vivid colors and a great marriage of flavors. Serve over rice or orzo pasta.

1 package (10 ounces) frozen spinach
1 cup white wine
2 garlic cloves, minced

1 large onion, chopped
1 can (16 ounces) plum tomatoes
16 ounces flounder

1. Preheat the oven to 350°F. In a medium-size saucepan, combine the spinach, wine, garlic, onion, and plum tomatoes. Bring to a simmer and break up the tomatoes and spinach with a wooden spoon. Simmer for 5 more minutes until the spinach is soft.

2. Pour the mixture into a baking dish and place the fish on top. Cover the dish with aluminum foil, crimping the sides. Bake for 20 minutes, or until the fish is done.

4 SERVINGS
PER SERVING: 175 Calories • 1.3 Grams Fat • 8.1% Calories from Fat

Sole with Shiitakes and Leeks

The earthy flavor of the mushrooms gives a whole new depth to the mild-mannered sole. Fresh shiitakes are available sometimes in better supermarkets, and their flavor can't be surpassed. (If you use them, omit the soaking.)

3 small leeks
$\frac{1}{4}$ cup white wine
$\frac{1}{2}$ cup vegetable broth

8 shiitakes, dried
1 tablespoon tamari soy sauce
16 ounces sole fillet

1. Slice the leeks in half lengthwise and rinse very well to remove all grit between the leaves. Drain the leeks and cut off the dark green leaves. Chop the remaining white and light-green parts.

2. Combine the white wine and vegetable broth and soak the mushrooms for 30 minutes. Remove the mushrooms, reserving the broth, and cut them into strips.

3. In a large skillet, combine the reserved wine and broth, mushrooms, leeks, and tamari sauce. Bring to a boil and reduce the heat. Simmer the leeks for 10 minutes, then place the sole fillets on top. Cover the pan and steam the fillets until they're done. Serve immediately.

4 SERVINGS
PER SERVING: 156 Calories • 1.3 Grams Fat • 7.6% Calories from Fat

Sole with Sun-Dried Tomatoes and Parsley

We wrap presents to sustain the suspense of the surprise a bit longer. It's worth the little extra effort to wrap the filling in the fish for the delight of finding the tomato, leek, and parsley.

1 cup parsley sprigs
$\frac{1}{4}$ cup plus 3 teaspoons white wine
$\frac{3}{4}$ cup minced leek, white part only
$\frac{1}{2}$ cup minced parsley
4 sun-dried tomatoes
16 ounces (4 fillets) sole

1. Preheat the oven to 375°F. In an ovenproof dish large enough to hold rolled-up fillets, add the parsley sprigs and the ¼ cup wine. Set aside.

2. In a small nonstick skillet, simmer the leeks and minced parsley in the 3 teaspoons of wine. In a small bowl pour hot water over the sun-dried tomatoes and let them soften for 10 minutes.

3. Spread out a fish fillet and on one end dollop one-quarter of the leek-parsley mixture and 1 sun-dried tomato. Roll the fillet and place it seam down in the prepared dish, on top of the bed of parsley. Repeat with the other 3 fillets.

4. Place aluminum foil over the dish and crimp the edges. Bake for 15 minutes, or until the fish flakes easily when a fork is inserted. Serve hot with some wine sauce over the fish.

4 SERVINGS
PER SERVING: 156 Calories • 1.5 Grams Fat • 8.6% Calories from Fat

Tuna Potato Cakes with Tartar Sauce

These patties can be made ahead of time and warmed up just before serving. This is true family fare and was given very high marks by adults and kids alike in my extended family.

1 can (6 ounces) tuna in water
2 cups boiled potatoes
3 egg whites (or 2 tablespoons pasteurized dried egg whites
plus 6 tablespoons water)
¾ cup matzo meal
1 medium onion, minced fine
½ cup finely minced celery
1 teaspoon dried sage
¼ teaspoon salt
½ teaspoon olive oil
1 cup nonfat mayonnaise
2 small shallots, minced
½ spear dill pickle, minced
1 tablespoon Dijon mustard
Salt and freshly ground black pepper

1. Drain the tuna. Mash the potatoes. In a mixing bowl, lightly beat the pasteurized dried egg whites. Add the tuna, potatoes, matzo meal, onion, celery, sage, and salt to the egg whites (or pasteurized dried egg whites and water) and combine thoroughly. Form 8 patties. Put them on a plate, cover and refrigerate for 30 minutes.

2. Meanwhile, make the tartar sauce by combining the mayonnaise with the shallots, pickle, and mustard. Add salt and pepper to taste. Refrigerate until ready to serve.

3. Coat the bottom of a nonstick pan with the oil and heat the pan for 20 seconds. Brown the patties over medium heat for 5 minutes. Turn them gently and brown the other side for 5 minutes, or until warmed through. Serve warm with tartar sauce.

4 SERVINGS
PER SERVING: 258 Calories • 1.6 Grams Fat • 5.6% Calories from Fat

Tuna Pasta

A family favorite, Tuna Pasta is simple enough for a child to make and flavorful enough for an adult to enjoy. It's also adaptable to include leftover vegetables or other herbs.

1 can (6 ounces) tuna in water
2 cups canned tomatoes, chopped
$\frac{1}{4}$ cup white wine
$\frac{1}{4}$ cup chopped fresh basil
1 teaspoon dried oregano
Salt and freshly ground black pepper
$\frac{3}{4}$ pound fettucini
2 tablespoons grated Parmesan cheese

1. Bring the tuna, tomatoes, wine, basil, and oregano to a boil in a saucepan. Simmer for 20 minutes, stirring occasionally. Add salt and pepper to taste.

2. Meanwhile, bring a large pot of water to a boil and cook the fettucini according to package directions. Drain.

3. Serve the pasta in a large, heated bowl with the tuna sauce over it. Sprinkle the cheese on top. Serve immediately.

4 SERVINGS
PER SERVING: 412 Calories • 2.8 Grams Fat • 6.3% Calories from Fat

Pasta Niçoise

Traditionally a Niçoise salad has tuna, green beans, olives, and many other vegetables served with a dressing. In this recipe the main ingredients find their way into a sauce that will stick to your ribs, not to your hips.

1 can (6 ounces) tuna in water
1 can (28 ounces) tomato puree
2 medium onions, diced
3 garlic cloves, minced
$\frac{1}{2}$ small sweet red pepper, diced
$\frac{1}{2}$ small sweet green pepper, diced
1 celery rib
8 green beans, chopped
1 tablespoon minced fresh thyme (or 1 teaspoon dried)
1 tablespoon minced fresh basil (or 1 teaspoon dried)
$\frac{1}{2}$ teaspoon apple-cider vinegar
1 pound ziti pasta
2 tablespoons minced parsley
8 green olives, sliced

1. In a medium-size saucepan, mix the tuna, tomato puree, onions, garlic, peppers, celery, green beans, thyme, basil, and vinegar. Bring to a boil, reduce the heat, and simmer for 25 minutes, stirring occasionally.
2. Meanwhile, bring a large pot of water to a rolling boil and boil the pasta until just done.
3. In a large, preheated serving bowl combine the pasta and the tuna sauce, and toss to combine. Sprinkle parsley and olives over all. Serve piping hot.

6 SERVINGS
PER SERVING: 435 Calories • 2.5 Grams Fat • 5.1% Calories from Fat

Linguini with Garlic Clam Sauce

This is an easy dish to prepare, and the presentation with the clams on top is very festive. If you love fresh clams, by all means use more of them.

$\frac{3}{4}$ pound linguini
8 littleneck clams
1 cup white wine
3 garlic cloves
1 can (13 ounces) minced clams, with liquid
$\frac{1}{4}$ cup water
2 tablespoons grated Parmesan cheese

1. Cook the linguini according to package directions. Scrub and clean the clams.

2. In a food processor or blender, combine ½ cup of the wine and the garlic. Process for 30 seconds, or until the garlic is very fine. Pour the garlic broth into a saucepan, add the minced clams with their liquid, and simmer gently for 10 minutes.

3. Pour the other ½ cup of wine plus the water into a separate saucepan and add the whole clams. Heat to a simmer, cover, and steam the clams for 5 to 10 minutes, or until they open. Discard any that fail to open.

4. Add the liquid from the clam pot to the garlic broth.

5. Place the drained linguini in a large heated bowl. Pour the clam sauce over it and sprinkle with the Parmesan cheese. Arrange the whole clams on top and serve immediately in deep plates.

4 SERVINGS
PER SERVING: 394 Calories • 2.4 Grams Fat • 6.2% Calories from Fat

Seafood Fettucini

This dish benefits from its simplicity—just fish and sauce over noodles with nothing else to distract your taste buds. Vary the seafood according to what is freshest in the market. If you stay with the low-fat varieties, you'll be in the ballpark of what's acceptable by our fat criterion.

$\frac{3}{4}$ pound fettucini
4 ounces haddock
4 ounces shrimp
4 ounces scallops
$\frac{3}{4}$ cup skim milk
$\frac{1}{4}$ cup white wine
1 cup clam juice
1 tablespoon flour
$\frac{1}{2}$ teaspoon vegetable-broth mix
$\frac{1}{2}$ teaspoon dried thyme
$\frac{1}{4}$ cup fresh parsley
1 tablespoon grated Parmesan cheese
Freshly ground black pepper

1. Cook the fettucini according to package directions.

2. Cut the fish into 1-inch pieces. Devein the shrimp and cut into smaller pieces if they're large. Halve or quarter the scallops. Set aside.

3. In a food processor or blender, combine the milk, wine, clam juice, flour, broth mix, and thyme. Process until smooth. Heat a large nonstick skillet for 20 seconds and add the blended milk mixture. Bring to a boil, stirring constantly. Reduce the heat and simmer gently for 2 minutes.

4. Add the fish and heat very gently for a few minutes, or until the fish is cooked.

5. Ladle the fettucini into a heated bowl and spoon the sauce over it. Sprinkle with the parsley and Parmesan. Grate pepper over individual servings to taste.

4 SERVINGS
PER SERVING: 464 Calories • 2.8 Grams Fat • 5.7% Calories from Fat

POULTRY

Not all chicken and turkey parts are created alike, and if you want to stick to getting less than 10 percent of your calories from fat, you'll have to confine yourself to skinless chicken breasts or turkey cutlets. Dark meat has too much fat—and skin is almost *all* fat! The wonderful thing about chicken is that it will adapt to almost any cuisine: From Italy to India, from France to Cuba, the chicken is always at home. Buy breasts in bulk when they're on sale and freeze them in the quantities you usually use them. If you learn to debone them yourself, you can save even more. Be sure to save the bones and make chicken soup: I deliberately leave on quite a bit of meat so that my soup will be rich.

Broccoli-Ginger Stir-Fry Chicken

Apart from the marinating time, this fast and easy Chinese meal can be on the table in the time it takes to cook the rice. Fresh ginger is essential for the taste of this dish, so don't use the powdered kind.

$1\frac{1}{2}$ pounds skinless chicken breasts
$\frac{1}{4}$ cup tamari soy sauce
$2\frac{1}{2}$ cups water
1 cup brown rice
8 cups broccoli florets
4 cups sliced mushrooms
4 scallions, minced
1 tablespoon grated fresh ginger

1. Cut the chicken into ½-inch strips. Place in a medium bowl and combine with the tamari and ¼ cup of water. Marinate for 1 hour.

2. In a saucepan, bring the remaining 2¼ cups water to boil. Stir in the rice, cover, and simmer for 45 minutes.

3. Using a steamer basket, lightly steam the broccoli until it's bright green. Set aside.

4. Heat a large, nonstick skillet and add the mushrooms. Keep the mushrooms moving with a wooden spoon until they're slightly brown and wilted. Add the scallions, ginger, and chicken with marinade. Simmer until the chicken strips are no longer pink.

5. Add the broccoli and mix well. Serve hot over the rice.

4 SERVINGS
PER SERVING: 271 calories • 3.1 Grams Fat • 9.5% Calories from Fat

Chicken in Three Onions

The fierce bite of onions is tempered by slow cooking, and a bit of wine mellows out the flavor even further. Use the soft green parts of the leeks and the scallions. Try this with Garlic Parmesan Mashed Potatoes (page 144).

3 medium leeks
4 scallions, chopped
1 small onion, chopped
$\frac{2}{3}$ cup white wine
$\frac{1}{4}$ teaspoon salt
$\frac{1}{4}$ cup nonfat sour cream
4 skinless chicken-breast halves, bone in

1. Cut the roots off the leeks and slice them in half lengthwise. Separate the leaves and wash them thoroughly to remove the soil most leeks have lodged between their leaves. Chop the leeks, and combine them with the scallions and onion. Place half the mixture in a skillet. Add the wine and salt.

2. Place the chicken breasts on top of the onion mixture, bone side down. Cover with the remaining onion mixture. Bring the liquid to a simmer and reduce the heat. Cover and let the chicken stew for 20 minutes, or until the meat is cooked.

3. Remove the chicken to a warm platter. Stir the sour cream into the onion mixture. Heat through for 1 minute but don't let it boil. Pour the mixture over and around the chicken on the platter. Serve warm.

4 SERVINGS
PER SERVING: 203 Calories • 1.6 Grams Fat • 8.3% Calories from Fat

Chicken and Peppers Kabobs

You can put lots of different vegetables on the grill, from onions to zucchini. And though the smell of food cooking on an outdoor grill is second to none, you can make these successfully in your broiler, too.

1 pound skinless chicken-breast halves
$\frac{1}{4}$ cup lime juice
3 tablespoons tamari soy sauce
3 tablespoons brown sugar
1 teaspoon powdered ginger
1 medium sweet red pepper
1 medium sweet green pepper
1 pint cherry tomatoes

1. Soak 8 wooden skewers in water for at least 30 minutes to prevent scorching. Preheat the broiler or prepare the grill.

2. Cut the chicken breasts into 1-inch squares. In a medium-size bowl, combine the lime juice, soy sauce, brown sugar, and ginger. Add the chicken cubes and marinate for 2 hours.

3. Remove the membranes from the peppers and cut into 1-inch pieces.

4. Arrange the chicken, peppers, and tomatoes alternately on the skewers. Broil the kabobs on the grill or under the broiler for about 5 minutes. Then turn and grill or broil until the chicken is done. Serve immediately.

4 SERVINGS
PER SERVING: 162 Calories • 1.5 Grams Fat • 8.2% Calories from Fat

Chicken à l'Orange

When I made this for my family, both adults and children couldn't get enough! The broiling caramelizes the juices just a tad and makes the sauce irrestible. Be sure to use fresh orange juice: The frozen variety will not reap comparable results.

3 oranges
1 medium onion, minced
1 garlic clove, minced
$\frac{1}{8}$ teaspoon salt
4 skinless, boneless chicken-breast halves
1 tablespoon Grand Marnier or other orange-flavored liqueur

1. Preheat the broiler. Squeeze the juice from two of the oranges. Peel the third and slice it into thin slices.

2. Combine the orange juice, onion, garlic, and salt in a large skillet and add the orange slices. Lay the chicken breasts on top and simmer for about 6 minutes. Add the Grand Marnier and simmer for another 2 minutes, or until the chicken is almost cooked throughout.

3. Transfer the chicken and sauce to an ovenproof dish and broil for 3 minutes, or until the edges of the chicken and the oranges get slightly burnt. Serve immediately.

4 SERVINGS
PER SERVING: 184 Calories • 1.7 Grams Fat • 7.8% Calories from Fat

Coq au Vin Blanc

This dish takes a full hour and a half to prepare and cook, but it's worth every minute of waiting. Fragrant and rich, it will satisfy you more than any high-fat stew possibly could.

4 skinless chicken-breast halves
3 medium potatoes, cubed
2 carrots, sliced
1 large onion, chopped
1 cup white wine
1 cup skim milk
2 tablespoons flour
1 teaspoon vegetable-broth mix
1½ teaspoons minced fresh thyme (or ½ teaspoon dried)
¼ teaspoon ground rosemary
5 ounces mushrooms, sliced

1. Cut the chicken-breast halves into thirds and place in a large pot. Add the potatoes, carrots, and onion. Set aside.

2. Place the wine, milk, flour, broth mix, thyme, and rosemary in a food processor or blender. Heat a large, nonstick skillet for 30 seconds. Process the wine mixture for 20 seconds and pour into the warm pan. Stir constantly over medium heat until the sauce comes to a full boil and thickens. Pour the sauce over the vegetables and chicken. Bring to a boil and simmer over very low heat for 1 hour, stirring occasionally.

3. After 1 hour, add the mushrooms and simmer covered for another 30 minutes. Stir occasionally to prevent scorching.

4. Serve piping hot in deep soup plates.

4 SERVINGS
PER SERVING: 282 Calories • 1.9 Grams Fat • 6.9% Calories from Fat

BBQ Chicken

No need to wait for summer. This indoor barbecue can be enjoyed anytime. Serve with Dijon Potato Salad (page 34), lemonade, and piles of napkins.

1 garlic clove, minced
1 cup canned tomatoes, crushed
$\frac{1}{3}$ cup apple juice
1 tablespoon cider vinegar
1 tablespoon minced onion
$\frac{1}{4}$ teaspoon ground ginger
4 skinless chicken-breast halves, bone in

1. Preheat the oven to 400°F.
2. In a saucepan, combine the garlic, tomatoes, apple juice, vinegar, onion, and ginger. Bring to a boil and simmer for 5 minutes, or until the sauce thickens.
3. Place the chicken on a baking dish, bone side down. Pour the sauce over the chicken and bake for 45 minutes, or until the chicken is done.
4. Heat up the broiler. Broil the chicken for 1 or 2 minutes to caramelize the sauce. Serve hot, warm, or cold.

4 SERVINGS
PER SERVING: 141 Calories • 1.5 Grams Fat • 10.0% Calories from Fat

Curry Chicken with Fig Pineapple Chutney

Your whole kitchen will be filled with the irresistible aroma of Indian spices when you make this. Prepare the chutney at least 1 hour before you cook the chicken. Cucumber Raita (page 132) and plain basmati rice are a good accompaniment.

Chutney Ingredients

3 ounces dried figs, chopped
6 pineapple rings, juice drained
Juice of $\frac{1}{2}$ lemon
1 tablespoon currants
1 tablespoon minced crystallized ginger
$\frac{1}{4}$ cup minced sweet red pepper
1 tablespoon tamari soy sauce
$\frac{1}{2}$ teaspoon coriander
$\frac{1}{4}$ teaspoon dry mustard
$\frac{1}{4}$ teaspoon cayenne pepper
$\frac{1}{4}$ teaspoon allspice

Chicken Ingredients

2 tablespoons curry powder
1 tablespoon cumin powder
16 ounces skinless chicken-breast halves, bone in
$\frac{3}{4}$ teaspoon olive oil
1 cup nonfat chicken broth
$\frac{1}{4}$ cup minced onion

1. To make the chutney, combine all the listed ingredients in a saucepan and simmer for 1 hour. Allow the mixture to cool before preparing the chicken.

2. To prepare the chicken, combine the curry and the cumin in a small bowl. Rub the mixture all over the chicken breasts.

3. Heat the oil in a nonstick skillet for 15 seconds. Add the chicken and brown over medium heat on one side for 3 minutes. Turn over and brown the other side for 3 minutes.

4. Add the chicken broth and onions and bring to a boil. Reduce the heat and simmer for 15 minutes, or until the breasts are cooked through. Serve with the room-temperature chutney on the side.

4 SERVINGS
PER SERVING: 430 Calories • 3.4 Grams Fat • 6.9% Calories from Fat

Provençal Chicken

A wonderfully fragrant, hearty meal. It's best when served with a hearty peasant bread.

1 cup white wine
2 garlic cloves, minced
1 medium onion, chopped
10 ounces mushrooms, sliced
1½ teaspoons minced fresh thyme
(or ½ teaspoon dried)
1½ teaspoons minced fresh rosemary
(or ½ teaspoon dried)

¼ cup plus 1 teaspoon chopped
fresh parsley
4 medium potatoes, diced
4 skinless, boneless chicken-breast
halves, cut into thirds
8 artichoke hearts, water packed
Salt and freshly ground black pepper

1. Combine the wine, garlic, onion, mushrooms, thyme, rosemary, and 1 teaspoon of the parsley in a large saucepan. Bring to a boil.
2. Add the potatoes, chicken, and artichoke hearts. Cover and simmer for 35 minutes. Add salt and pepper to taste.
3. Serve in large soup bowls. Sprinkle with the remaining ¼ cup parsley.

4 SERVINGS
PER SERVING: 343 Calories • 2.1 Grams Fat • 6.0% Calories from Fat

Scallion Mustard Chicken

This is good company fare without being fussy. It's great with steamed broccoli and eggless noodles.

3 scallions
3 tablespoons lemon juice
1 tablespoon coarse Dijon mustard
2 garlic cloves

1 tablespoon honey cream
½ teaspoon salt
4 skinless chicken-breast halves, bone in

1. Cut the scallions into 2-inch pieces, using green and white parts. In a food processor or blender place the lemon juice, mustard, garlic, honey cream, and salt. Puree.
2. Spread the scallion-mustard mixture over the chicken. Refrigerate, covered, for 1 hour.
3. Preheat oven to 350°F. Put the chicken and marinade in an ovenproof dish. Bake for 40 minutes, or until cooked through.

4 SERVINGS
PER SERVING: 152 Calories • 1.7 Grams Fat • 10.0% Calories from Fat

Tarragon Chicken

I first enjoyed chicken in tarragon sauce at an elegant wedding dinner held in a European castle. Its taste has intrigued me ever since. Make this dish for a candlelit dinner—or just because.

4 skinless chicken-breast halves, bone in
$\frac{1}{2}$ cup skim milk
$\frac{1}{2}$ cup white wine
1 tablespoon flour
1 tablespoon vegetable-broth mix
$\frac{1}{4}$ teaspoon salt
1 scallion, minced
1 tablespoon minced fresh tarragon

1. Coat a nonstick skillet with cooking spray and heat for 1 minute. Place the chicken, meaty side down, in the skillet and brown for about 3 minutes. Turn and brown the other side for 3 additional minutes. Remove the chicken and set aside.

2. Place the milk, wine, flour, broth mix, and salt in a blender and process until smooth. Pour immediately into the warm skillet and heat to boiling, stirring constantly. When the sauce thickens, add the scallion. Mix well and return the chicken to the skillet breast side down. Add the tarragon. Cover and simmer for 10 minutes.

3. Turn the chicken, cover, and simmer for another 5 minutes, or until the chicken is cooked. Spoon the sauce over the chicken and serve.

4 SERVINGS
PER SERVING: 172 Calories • 1.5 Grams Fat • 9.2% Calories from Fat

Apple-Cider Chicken

I make this every fall, when the first cider comes off the local presses. You can make this with bottled juice, but for the full flavor impact, use the real thing.

1 Granny Smith apple
1 cup apple cider
2 teaspoons grated fresh ginger
4 skinless chicken-breast halves, bone in
1½ cups sliced mushrooms
1½ teaspoons minced fresh thyme (or ½ teaspoon dried)
2 tablespoons nonfat sour cream
Salt and freshly ground black pepper

1. Quarter and core the apple and cut each quarter into 3 slices. Mix the cider with the ginger and set aside.

2. Coat a nonstick skillet with cooking spray. Heat for 30 seconds. Place the chicken breasts in the skillet, flesh side down, and brown for 3 minutes. Turn and brown the other side for 3 more minutes.

3. Pour the cider over the chicken. Add the apple and mushroom slices to the skillet and sprinkle the thyme over all. Bring to a boil. Reduce the heat and simmer for 15 minutes, or until done.

4. Remove the chicken to a heated platter. Add the sour cream to the sauce, mix well, and heat gently without letting it boil. Add salt and pepper to taste. Pour the sauce over the chicken and serve immediately.

4 SERVINGS
PER SERVING: 182 Calories • 1.6 Grams Fat • 8.2% Calories from Fat

Chicken, Spinach, and Rice Avgolemono

For years I read about Avgolemono recipes in Greek cookbooks and hesitated to make them. Mixing egg and lemon into a savory dish wasn't something my mouth could imagine. Oh, the years I wasted with my timidity!

1 medium onion, chopped
2 cups chicken broth
1 cup white rice
$1\frac{1}{2}$ teaspoons minced fresh oregano (or $\frac{1}{2}$ teaspoon dried)
4 skinless chicken-breast halves, bone in
1 package (10 ounces) frozen spinach, thawed
1 tablespoon snipped fresh dill
$\frac{1}{4}$ cup fresh lemon juice
$\frac{1}{2}$ cup water
2 teaspoons all-purpose flour
2 teaspoons pasteurized dried egg whites
1 tablespoon grated Parmesan cheese

1. Preheat the broiler. In a large nonstick skillet combine the onion, broth, rice, and oregano. Stir well and bring to a boil. Place the chicken breasts on top, cover, and simmer for 15 minutes.

2. Remove the chicken and set aside. Add the spinach and dill and mix well. Place the chicken on top of the mixture, cover, and simmer for 5 more minutes.

3. In a small bowl, combine the lemon juice, water, flour and pasteurized dried egg whites. Again remove the chicken from the skillet and set aside. Add the lemon-juice mixture to the rice and stir until the juice is absorbed.

4. Place the chicken on the broiler rack and sprinkle the Parmesan cheese over it. Broil for 1 or 2 minutes, or until the chicken gets some color. Place the chicken on top of the rice and serve hot.

4 SERVINGS
PER SERVING: 348 Calories • 3.4 Grams Fat • 8.9% Calories from Fat

Yogurt Curry Chicken and Basmati Rice

Garam masala is an Indian spice blend that you can purchase prepared or make yourself in a spice grinder or clean coffee grinder. You'll have some extra, which will keep for a month or two in a tightly closed jar.

Garam Masala Ingredients

1 teaspoon cumin

$\frac{1}{8}$ teaspoon cayenne

1 cinnamon stick

5 whole cloves

$\frac{1}{2}$ teaspoon peppercorns

$\frac{1}{4}$ teaspoon freshly ground nutmeg

$\frac{1}{4}$ teaspoon whole coriander seed

$\frac{1}{2}$ teaspoon turmeric

Chicken Ingredients

1 cup nonfat yogurt

2 small onions

Juice of $\frac{1}{2}$ lemon

1 teaspoon grated fresh ginger

2 garlic cloves

4 skinless chicken-breast halves, bone in

2 cups water

1 cup basmati rice

1 cup frozen peas

$\frac{1}{4}$ teaspoon salt

1. Grind together the cumin, cayenne, cinnamon stick, cloves, peppercorns, nutmeg, coriander, and turmeric in a spice blender or coffee grinder. Set aside.
2. Combine the yogurt, 1 onion, lemon juice, ginger, and garlic in a food processor or blender. Process until smooth. Add 1¼ teaspoons of the spice mixture and blend again.
3. Put the chicken breasts in a mixing bowl and pour the yogurt mixture over them. Stir well. Refrigerate for 2 hours.
4. Arrange the chicken and marinade in a single layer in a large, nonstick skillet. Simmer for 20 minutes, or until the chicken is cooked.
5. While the chicken cooks, chop the second onion and bring the water to a boil. Add the rice and chopped onion. Return to a boil. Cover, reduce the heat, and simmer for 20 minutes. When the rice is done, add the frozen peas and heat them through for 1 minute. Arrange the rice on a large platter and place the chicken and sauce in the middle. The rice will absorb the curdled yogurt, and it won't show.

4 SERVINGS
PER SERVING: 414 Calories • 3.9 Grams Fat • 8.3% Calories from Fat

Sweet and Sour Chicken with Rice

This is a melting-pot recipe: A Chinese dish that has become completely Americanized. And as much as I love eating the authentic food, I also believe there's a place for these New World adaptations.

2 cups water
$\frac{1}{4}$ teaspoon salt
1 cup basmati rice
1 medium onion, chopped
2 garlic cloves, minced
1 tablespoon brown sugar
2 tablespoons apple-cider vinegar
$\frac{1}{2}$ teaspoon fresh grated ginger
1 cup chicken broth
3 tomatoes
1 large sweet green pepper
4 skinless, boneless chicken breasts cut in 1-inch chunks
1 cup frozen green peas
$\frac{1}{2}$ teaspoon cornstarch

1. In a medium-size saucepan boil the water with the salt. Add the rice. Stir and reduce heat. Cover and let simmer for 20 minutes.

2. Coat a nonstick skillet with cooking spray and heat for 30 seconds. Add the onion and brown for 3 minutes. Add the garlic, brown sugar, vinegar, and ginger. Cook for 3 minutes. Add the broth, tomatoes, and green pepper and simmer for 3 minutes.

3. Add the chicken and simmer for 5 minutes. Add the peas and cook for 2 more minutes, or until the chicken is cooked through.

4. Remove the chicken and vegetables from the skillet and arrange them on a heated platter. Bring the broth to a boil. In a cup, dissolve the cornstarch in 1 tablespoon of cold water and add to the boiling broth. Stir until the broth thickens, then cook for 1 minute.

5. Pour the sauce over the chicken and vegetables and serve over hot rice.

4 SERVINGS
PER SERVING: 381 Calories • 2.8 Grams Fat • 6.7% Calories from Fat

Chicken with Roasted Shallots and Rice

Add to this delicious dish a vegetable, and you have a complete meal. Roasted shallots are sweet and succulent, just as roasted garlic cloves are.

12 shallots
2 cups water
$\frac{1}{2}$ teaspoon salt
1 cup rice
$\frac{1}{4}$ teaspoon ground cardamom
$\frac{1}{4}$ teaspoon cumin powder
$\frac{1}{2}$ cup minced red pepper
$1\frac{1}{2}$ cups cooked chicken, cubed
$\frac{1}{4}$ cup minced fresh parsley

1. Preheat the oven to 350°F. Break the shallots apart, but do not remove their skins. Place in an ovenproof dish and bake for 20 minutes, or until soft when pierced. Cool and remove the skins.
2. Mince 4 of the cloves. Place the rest at the edge of a serving plate.
3. Bring the water and salt to a boil in a medium-size saucepan. Add the rice, cardamom, and cumin, and return to a boil. Stir, cover, and simmer for 10 minutes.
4. Add the red pepper to the rice and stir. Simmer, covered, for 10 more minutes, or until the rice is done. Add the chicken and minced shallots and heat through. Add the parsley and mix. Mound the rice on the center of the serving plate with the roasted shallots. Serve warm.

6 SERVINGS
PER SERVING: 209 Calories • 1.9 Grams Fat • 8.2% Calories from Fat

Chicken Ragout

This is a no-apology way to use up some cooked chicken and potatoes. Robust and hearty, this dish is best when served with hunks of bread, stoneground mustard, and a glass of red wine.

1 medium onion, chopped
2 cups chopped Portabella mushrooms
2 garlic cloves, minced
$\frac{1}{2}$ cup red wine
2 medium tomatoes, chopped
$1\frac{1}{2}$ cups cooked and cubed skinless chicken-breast halves
$1\frac{1}{2}$ cups cooked and cubed red potatoes
$1\frac{1}{2}$ cups frozen artichokes
1 tablespoon minced fresh oregano

1. Coat a large nonstick skillet with cooking spray. Heat for 30 seconds. Add the onion and sauté, stirring, for 2 minutes. Add the mushrooms and stir until they have given up most of their moisture and are limp. Add the garlic and heat for 1 more minute.

2. Add the wine, tomatoes, chicken, potatoes, artichokes, and oregano and simmer for 10 minutes. Serve hot.

4 SERVINGS
PER SERVING: 163 Calories • 1.5 Grams Fat • 8.9% Calories from Fat

Red Hot Cuban Chicken and Rice

When I lived on the Upper West Side of Manhattan, my street bordered a Spanish neighborhood. This chicken reminds me of the good food that was there—except this version is a lot less fattening.

2 tablespoons paprika
$\frac{1}{4}$ teaspoon cayenne
$\frac{1}{4}$ teaspoon salt
4 skinless chicken-breast halves
$\frac{3}{4}$ teaspoon olive oil
4 garlic cloves, minced
1 medium onion, chopped
3 cups nonfat chicken broth
1 cup white rice
$\frac{1}{2}$ cup minced fresh cilantro

1. In a small bowl, mix the paprika, cayenne, and salt. Rub the spice mixture all over the chicken.

2. Heat the oil in a nonstick skillet. Add the chicken pieces and brown them, skin side down, for 2 minutes. Turn the chicken over and brown for 2 more minutes. Remove the chicken and set aside.

3. Add the garlic and onion to the skillet and cook for 1 minute, stirring constantly. Carefully add the broth and rice and stir. Place the chicken on top and bring to a boil. Cover the skillet and simmer for 30 minutes, or until the chicken and the rice are cooked. Serve with the cilantro sprinkled on top.

4 SERVINGS
PER SERVING: 332 Calories • 3.1 Grams Fat • 8.5% Calories from Fat

Maple Ginger Chicken

This sweet chicken tastes best when accompanied by plain rice and steamed broccoli. Be sure to use real maple syrup and fresh orange juice for best flavor.

⅓ cup maple syrup
½ cup fresh orange juice
1 shallot, minced

1 teaspoon minced fresh ginger
4 skinless chicken-breast halves, bone in

1. In a skillet, combine the maple syrup, orange juice, shallot, and ginger. Place the chicken in the sauce and bring to a boil. Reduce the heat, cover, and simmer for 15 minutes, occasionally spooning the sauce over the chicken.

2. Preheat the broiler. Place the chicken on a broiler pan and broil for 4 minutes, or until the chicken is cooked and slightly browned.

4 SERVINGS
PER SERVING: 212 Calories • 1.5 Grams Fat • 6.7% Calories from Fat

Lemon Chicken

Lemon is a wonderful flavoring for a low-fat diet. Combine it with chicken, and you have a mouth-watering entrée. This lemony marinade can also be used for barbecued chicken.

4 skinless, boneless chicken-breast halves
1 lemon
¼ cup nonfat chicken broth

½ teaspoon grated ginger
Pinch of cayenne
4 sprigs parsley

1. Place the chicken cutlets between two pieces of waxed paper and flatten with a wooden mallet or use the side of a small can.

2. Cut the lemon in half. Squeeze the juice from half the lemon and cut 2 strips of the zest. Cut 4 thin slices from the other half and set aside for garnish.

3. In a small saucepan, combine the broth, lemon juice, zest, ginger, and cayenne. Bring to a boil and simmer for 5 minutes. Let cool. Place the chicken cutlets in a self-sealing bag. Add the marinade and refrigerate for at least 1 hour.

4. Remove the marinated breasts from the bag. Coat a nonstick skillet with cooking spray and heat for 20 seconds. Add the chicken breasts, browning them quickly on both sides. Garnish with parsley sprigs and lemon slices and serve immediately.

4 SERVINGS
PER SERVING: 318 Calories • 4.4 Grams Fat • 10.0% Calories from Fat

Lemon Caper Chicken in Clay Pot

Clay-pot cooking steams the flavor into the food, making this chicken lemony and tart.
As a bonus, you get a broth that is delicious on plain rice or Garlic Parmesan
Mashed Potatoes (page 144).

1 lemon
4 skinless chicken-breast halves, bone in
$\frac{1}{2}$ teaspoon salt
$\frac{1}{4}$ teaspoon freshly ground black pepper
3 small onions, sliced
2 tablespoons capers
$\frac{1}{2}$ cup white wine
$\frac{1}{4}$ cup nonfat chicken broth
1 bay leaf
$\frac{1}{2}$ teaspoon dried thyme (or 1 teaspoon fresh thyme)

1. Make sure the oven is off and cold. Soak the unglazed clay pot in water for 15 minutes. Drain.

2. Cut the lemon in half. Squeeze half and reserve the juice. Cut the other half into slices and reserve. Sprinkle the chicken with the salt and pepper and set aside.

3. Spread one third of the sliced onions in the bottom of the clay pot. Place 2 chicken breasts on top. Spread the next one third of the onions on the chicken and sprinkle 1 of the tablespoons of capers over the top. Place the next 2 chicken breasts over this and top with the last of the onions and capers. Pour the lemon juice, wine, and broth over all and stick the bay leaf in the liquid on the side of the pot. Sprinkle the thyme over all.

4. Cover the pot and place in a cold oven. Turn the oven to 475°F and bake for 1 hour. Serve hot.

4 SERVINGS
PER SERVING: 168 Calories • 1.5 Grams Fat • 9.7% Calories from Fat

Apple Sauerkraut Chicken in a Clay Pot

I seldom really love sauerkraut, but this is one exception. It gives up its bite for mellowness with the apples and wine and becomes irresistible: This dish is an Old-World delicacy. Serve this with a mashed potato, so you can enjoy all the broth and vegetables.

4 medium chicken-breast halves without skin
Salt and freshly ground black pepper
1 large apple, peeled, chopped
5 ounces mushrooms, sliced
1 small onion, sliced
1 cup sauerkraut
$\frac{1}{2}$ cup white wine
$\frac{1}{4}$ cup apple cider
1$\frac{1}{2}$ teaspoons minced fresh thyme (or $\frac{1}{2}$ teaspoon dried)

1. Make sure the oven is off and cold. Soak the unglazed cooking pot in water for 15 minutes. Drain.

2. Rub the chicken breasts with salt and pepper to taste. In a large bowl combine the apple, mushrooms, onion, and sauerkraut.

3. In the bottom of the clay pot spread the sauerkraut mixture. Arrange the chicken breasts on top. Pour the wine and apple cider over all. Sprinkle the chicken with thyme and additional pepper to taste.

4. Cover the pot and place in a cold oven. Turn the oven to 450°F and cook for 1 hour and 10 minutes. Serve hot.

4 SERVINGS
PER SERVING: 193 Calories • 1.8 Grams Fat • 9.1% Calories from Fat

Chicken with Herbed Vegetables in a Clay Pot

The fresh herbs used in this recipe should be seen as mere suggestions. Use whatever herbs are fresh in the garden or store and you can't go wrong. You can also substitute other vegetables, such as red or green peppers, zucchini, or sweet potatoes. Think of this as a generic clay-pot recipe: A few chicken breasts, a couple of cups of vegetables, a handful of herbs, a scant cup of liquid, and an hour later you have dinner on the table.

4 medium skinless chicken-breast halves
Salt and freshly ground black pepper
2 medium onions, sliced
1 cup sliced carrots
1 cup sliced celery
1 cup sliced mushrooms
2 garlic cloves, minced
1 tablespoon minced fresh parsley
1 teaspoon minced fresh oregano
1 teaspoon minced fresh basil
$\frac{3}{4}$ cup nonfat chicken broth
1 teaspoon balsamic vinegar

1. Make sure the oven is off and cold. Soak the unglazed clay pot in water for 15 minutes. Drain.
2. Sprinkle the chicken breasts with salt and pepper to taste and set aside. In a large bowl, combine the onions, carrots, celery, mushrooms, garlic, parsley, oregano, and basil and mix.
3. Spread one third of the herbed vegetables in the bottom of the clay pot. Top with 2 chicken breasts. Top them with the next third of the vegetables and place the last 2 chicken breasts on the vegetables. Top with the last of the vegetables. Pour the broth mixture over all, taking care not to wash the herbs off the vegetables.
4. Cover the pot and place it in the cold oven. Turn the heat to 475°F and bake for 1 hour.

4 SERVINGS
PER SERVING: 162 Calories • 1.6 Grams Fat • 9.3% Calories from Fat

Chicken with Potatoes and Peppers in Wine

This is a one-pot meal, needing only a simple salad. It's difficult to convey how these simple ingredients can make such magic in a clay pot, but they definitely do! The garlic cloves are rendered mild, so if you wish, put additional cloves in the pot. You can remove them and eat them separately spread on bread.

4 medium skinless chicken-breast halves
Salt and freshly ground black pepper
$2\frac{1}{2}$ cups cubed red potatoes
1 large sweet red pepper
8 garlic cloves
$\frac{3}{4}$ cup white wine
2 scallions, minced
1 tablespoon minced fresh oregano

1. Make sure the oven is off and cold. Soak the unglazed clay pot in water for 15 minutes. Drain.
2. Rub the chicken breasts with salt and pepper to taste. Cut the red pepper in half, remove the seeds, and slice into strips. Spread the pepper strips, potatoes, garlic, and wine in the bottom of the clay pot. Place the chicken on top of the vegetables and sprinkle the scallions and oregano over all.
3. Cover the pot and place in a cold oven. Turn the oven to 450°F and bake for 1 hour and 15 minutes. Serve hot.

4 SERVINGS
PER SERVING: 199 Calories • 1.6 Grams Fat • 8.5% Calories from Fat

Chicken Burgers

Hamburgers are often the only thing people who give up beef miss and yearn for. Serve chicken burgers the way you like hamburgers, with your choice of tomatoes, lettuce, pickles, ketchup, and nonfat mayonnaise. You'll never miss the beef!

1 large skinless chicken-breast half   1 tablespoon minced fresh parsley
1 tablespoon nonfat saltine-cracker crumbs   Salt and freshly ground black pepper
1 tablespoon white wine

1. Debone the chicken breast and remove all tendons. Place the chicken meat in a food processor and process with the steel blade, pulsing on and off, until ground.
2. Add the cracker crumbs, wine, parsley, and salt and pepper to taste. Mix well. Shape the ground-meat mixture into thin patties.
3. Coat a nonstick skillet with cooking spray and heat for 30 seconds. Place patties in skillet and fry for 1 or 2 minutes. (The chicken meat will cook quickly.) Turn the patty over and cook until completely done. Serve hot.

2 SERVINGS
PER SERVING: 94 Calories • 0.7 Gram Fat • 7.6% Calories from Fat

Chicken Fruit Salad

This fresh and fast salad gets a little twist from the roasted red peppers. Serve with warm French bread and a glass of iced tea on the patio.

2 teaspoons Dijon mustard
$\frac{1}{4}$ cup nonfat mayonnaise
$1\frac{1}{2}$ cups skinless chicken breasts, cooked and cubed
1 cup pineapple chunks in juice, drained
1 cup cubed cantaloupe
$\frac{1}{2}$ cup diced roasted red peppers
$\frac{1}{4}$ head Boston lettuce

1. In a large mixing bowl, combine the mustard and mayonnaise. Add the chicken, pineapple, and cantaloupe and mix well. Add the red peppers and stir lightly.
2. Arrange the lettuce leaves around the edge of a serving platter with the chicken salad in the center. Serve cold.

4 SERVINGS
PER SERVING: 144 Calories • 1.2 Grams Fat • 7.4% Calories from Fat

Fajitas

Sometimes it comes as a surprise to me—even after experimenting with so very many different foods—how easy it can be to make a delicious, healthful version of a food I know can be a fat counter's nightmare. Fajitas are a good example. Omitting the high-fat fillings, such as sour cream and avocado, and boosting the seasonings eliminates fat grams without compromising flavor.

4 skinless, boneless chicken-breast halves
$\frac{1}{4}$ cup lemon juice
1 teaspoon ground cumin
1 tablespoon minced fresh oregano or 1 teaspoon dried
Salt and freshly ground black pepper
1 sweet red pepper
1 sweet green pepper
1 large onion
Hot sauce
8 nonfat flour tortillas

1. Cut the chicken breasts into strips. In a shallow bowl, combine the lemon juice, cumin, oregano, and salt and pepper to taste. Add the chicken and marinate for 1 hour.

2. Coat a nonstick skillet with cooking spray and heat for 30 seconds. Add the chicken strips and cook them through, stirring constantly. Remove and set aside.

3. Core and seed the peppers and cut them into strips. Slice the onion and then cut the slices in half. In the skillet cook the onions and peppers while stirring constantly. When the onions start to brown, add the chicken and cook until heated through. Add hot sauce to taste.

4. Warm the tortillas according to the package directions. Spoon the chicken-and-peppers mixture on the heated tortillas and roll up. Serve immediately.

4 SERVINGS
PER SERVING: 266 Calories • 1.6 Grams Fat • 5.6% Calories from Fat

Turkey Cutlets with Apple Sage Stuffing

This is for those non-Thanksgiving days when you have an unexpected craving for turkey with stuffing. For an authentic experience, pair this with Cranberry Apple Sauce and Brussels Sprouts (pages 155 and 129).

2 cups bread cubes
½ cup chopped onion
1 stalk celery, chopped
½ cup sliced crimini mushrooms
1 apple, chopped

¼ cup nonfat chicken broth
½ teaspoon dried sage
1 pound skinless turkey cutlets, light meat
Salt and freshly ground black pepper

1. Preheat the oven to 375°F. Spread the bread cubes on a baking sheet and toast in the oven for 10 minutes, or until lightly browned. Set aside.
2. Coat a nonstick skillet with cooking spray and heat for 30 seconds. Add the onion and celery and brown for 3 minutes stirring constantly. Add the mushrooms and apples and stir for 2 more minutes. Stir in the broth and sage and simmer until the broth is almost all evaporated and the celery is soft.
3. Meanwhile, coat a nonstick skillet with cooking spray and heat for 20 seconds. Season the turkey cutlets with salt and pepper to taste and place them in a single layer in the hot pan. Brown on both sides.
4. Just before serving, toss the toasted bread cubes with the moist dressing and serve the cutlets with the bread mixture on the side. Serve immediately.

4 SERVINGS
PER SERVING: 352 Calories • 3.5 Grams Fat • 9.1% Calories from Fat

Turkey Cutlets with Roasted Shallot Sauce

Roasted shallot sauce spooned over turkey gives all the satisfaction of turkey with gravy without the fat. Serve with a few steamed red potatoes and Snow Peas and Carrots (page 130).

10 shallots
1 pound skinless light turkey meat cutlets
½ cup nonfat chicken broth
¼ cup white wine
1 tablespoon all-purpose flour
1½ teaspoons minced fresh thyme (or ½ teaspoon diced)
Salt and freshly ground black pepper

1. Preheat the oven to 350°F. Break the shallots apart but do not remove their skins. Place in an ovenproof dish and bake for 20 minutes or until soft when pierced. Cool and remove the skins.

2. Meanwhile, season the turkey cutlets with salt and pepper to taste.

3. Place the shallots, broth, wine, flour, and thyme in a food processor or blender and puree. Heat a nonstick skillet. Add the puree and stir constantly until thick. Simmer for 1 more minute. Add salt and pepper to taste and keep warm.

4. Coat a second nonstick skillet with cooking spray and heat for 20 seconds. Add the seasoned turkey cutlets and brown one side. Turn and continue to cook until done. Spoon the hot shallot sauce over the cutlets and serve.

4 SERVINGS
PER SERVING: 153 Calories • 1.3 Grams Fat • 8.6% Calories from Fat

VEGETARIAN MAIN DISHES _____

Vegetarian cooking has come of age. No longer is it full of the fat-laden, cheesy recipes of the sixties and seventies. Today's vegetarian diet relies on fresh vegetables, fruits, hearty grains, beans, and rice for substance and taste, and looks to herbs, spices, and low-fat hard cheeses for flavor.

Pasta with Fresh Tomatoes and Basil

The essence of summertime: red-ripe tomatoes at their peak, fresh aromatic basil, and just a hint of Parmesan. If you read this recipe in the middle of winter, anticipate and wait for tomatoes to ripen—and write yourself a note so you'll remember it, come summer.

1 pound fresh pasta
3 medium ripe tomatoes
$\frac{1}{4}$ cup fresh basil leaves, whole
$\frac{1}{4}$ cup nonfat mayonnaise
2 teaspoons balsamic vinegar
2 teaspoons Dijon mustard
$\frac{1}{4}$ teaspoon salt
Freshly ground black pepper
1 tablespoon grated Parmesan cheese

1. Cook the pasta according to package directions.
2. Meanwhile, dice the tomatoes and place them in a colander to drain. Roll each basil leaf so that it looks like a straw; slice very thinly.
3. In a small mixing bowl, combine the mayonnaise, vinegar, mustard, and salt. Blend well.
4. When the pasta is done, drain it and place in a large, heated serving bowl. Spoon the tomatoes, basil, and dressing over the top and mix well with two large spoons. Sprinkle pepper to taste and Parmesan cheese over individual portions.

4 SERVINGS
PER SERVING: 365 Calories • 3.4 Grams Fat • 8.3% Calories from Fat

Pasta with Sun-Dried Tomato Sauce

*Sun-dried tomatoes have a compelling, sweet, tangy flavor,
which stars in this quick and simple sauce.*

3 ounces dehydrated sun-dried tomatoes
2 cups nonfat vegetable or chicken broth
$\frac{1}{4}$ cup minced fresh basil

8 ounces fusilli
2 tablespoons grated Parmesan cheese

1. In a saucepan, simmer the tomatoes and broth for 15 minutes, or until the tomatoes are soft. Meanwhile, heat a large pot of water for the pasta.

2. Cool the tomatoes slightly. Place them in a blender with the broth, add the basil, and process until smooth. Pour the mixture back into the saucepan and heat through.

3. Cook the pasta according to package directions. Drain and place in a heated serving bowl. Spoon the sauce over the hot pasta and sprinkle with the Parmesan cheese.

4 SERVINGS
PER SERVING: 285 Calories • 2.3 Grams Fat • 7.1% Calories from Fat

Pasta in Herbed Tomato Sauce

*Fresh herbs make all the difference in this sauce. Fortunately,
the better food stores now carry fresh herbs year-round.*

3 cups tomato puree
$\frac{1}{2}$ cup onion
1 garlic clove
$\frac{1}{2}$ cup fresh parsley plus
3 sprigs for garnish

$\frac{1}{3}$ cup fresh oregano
Salt and freshly ground black pepper
3 cups pasta
2 tablespoons grated Parmesan cheese

1. Heat a large pot of water for the pasta. In a food processor or blender combine 2 cups of the tomato puree, the onion, and the garlic. Process until smooth. Pour the mixture into a saucepan and simmer for 30 minutes. Add salt and pepper to taste.

2. Blend the remaining cup of tomato puree with the parsley and oregano until the herbs are little flecks. Add this to the sauce and simmer for 5 more minutes.

3. Cook the pasta according to the package instructions.

4. Place the drained, hot pasta in a heated serving bowl. Pour the sauce over, sprinkle with the cheese, and garnish with the parsley sprigs.

4 SERVINGS
PER SERVING: 523 Calories • 4.7 Grams Fat • 7.5% Calories from Fat

Pasta with Triple Pepper Sauce

By now we all know that the fat calories are not in the pasta but in the sauces. If you make your sauces extra lean, you can top them with some grated Parmesan for a treat.

1 pound fresh pasta
1 sweet red pepper
1 sweet green pepper
1 sweet yellow pepper
1 medium onion, chopped
3 garlic cloves, minced
1 teaspoon minced fresh oregano
$\frac{1}{2}$ cup nonfat vegetable or chicken broth
1 cup tomato puree
Salt and freshly ground black pepper
3 tablespoons grated Parmesan cheese

1. Heat a large pot of water for the pasta. Meanwhile, core and seed the peppers and cut them into strips.

2. In a large nonstick skillet, combine the peppers, onion, garlic, oregano, and broth. Cover and simmer for 7 minutes.

3. Add the tomato puree to the skillet and heat through. Add salt and pepper to taste.

4. Cook the pasta according to the package instructions, drain, and place in a large, heated bowl. Pour the pepper sauce over the top and sprinkle with the cheese.

4 SERVINGS
PER SERVING: 371 Calories • 2.8 Grams Fat • 6.8% Calories from Fat

Pasta with Asparagus and Sun-Dried Tomatoes

An easy, fresh, springtime dish. Enjoy the first asparagus with a deep red tomato sauce. Invite a few friends over and dig in!

14 pieces sun-dried tomatoes
30 stalks asparagus
8 ounces sausage-flavored soy meat substitute
3 cups pasta shells
2 tablespoons grated Parmesan cheese
Freshly ground black pepper

1. Soak the sun-dried tomatoes in 1 cup of water for 15 minutes, or until the tomatoes are soft and pliable. Pour the tomatoes and the water into a food processor or blender and process until smooth.

2. Snap the woody, hard ends off the asparagus and cut the spears in 1-inch pieces. Place in a steamer basket and steam until bright green. Set aside.

3. Heat a nonstick skillet for 20 seconds and add the meat substitute. Cook, while breaking up the meat substitute with the end of a wooden spoon.

4. Cook the pasta according to package instructions. Arrange the timing so that the pasta, asparagus, and meat substitute are done at the same time.

5. Mix the hot, drained pasta, asparagus, and meat substitute together with the tomato sauce in a warm serving bowl. Sprinkle the cheese over the top and grind pepper to taste over all.

8 SERVINGS
PER SERVING: 230 Calories • 1.5 Grams Fat • 5.7% Calories from Fat

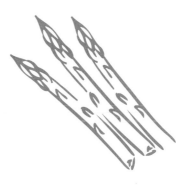

Risotto with Saffron and Sun-Dried Tomatoes

The trick to good risotto is not to be in a hurry: You must gently and patiently stir and keep adding hot broth—and stir some more—until all the liquid is incorporated. It's the perfect thing to do if a dear friend or loved one insists on telling you every detail of his or her latest adventure. You are going nowhere for about half an hour anyway, and when the story is over, you've this delicious meal to share.

$\frac{3}{4}$ cup chopped onion
2 garlic cloves, minced
1 cup arborio rice
$\frac{1}{2}$ cup white wine
Pinch of saffron
2 cups nonfat vegetable or chicken broth
1 cup water
8 pieces dehydrated sun-dried tomatoes, cut into pieces
2 tablespoons grated Parmesan cheese

1. Coat a nonstick skillet with cooking spray. Heat the pan for 20 seconds and add the onion. Brown the onion, stirring frequently. When it starts to take on color, add the garlic. Brown for 1 more minute and remove from the heat. Set aside.

2. Pour the broth and water into a saucepan. Bring to simmer and keep hot. Combine the rice, white wine, and saffron in a second saucepan. Turn on the heat and start to stir. Stir until the wine is incorporated. Add the onions and sun-dried tomatoes and ¼ cup of the hot broth mixture. Stir constantly until the broth is incorporated. Keep adding small amounts of broth and stirring until all the broth is incorporated and the rice is soft. The result you're after is creamy, al dente rice.

3. Place the risotto in a warm bowl and sprinkle with the Parmesan. Serve immediately.

4 SERVINGS
PER SERVING: 250 Calories • 1.2 Grams Fat • 4.7% Calories from Fat

Couscous

Couscous is a meal that lends itself to endless variation. You can add small quantities of leftover vegetables to this dish—pieces of cooked squash would be especially appropriate. This version is mild enough for just about anybody. Add more cayenne if you like the fire.

1 large onion, chopped
3 garlic cloves, minced
1 large sweet red pepper, chopped
1 large carrot, chopped
1½ cups canned chickpeas, drained
⅓ cup vegetable or chicken bouillon

⅓ cup raisins
½ teaspoon ground cumin
½ teaspoon ground coriander
¼ teaspoon cayenne
¼ cup minced fresh cilantro
6 cups cooked couscous

1. In a large saucepan, place the onion, garlic, red pepper, carrot, chickpeas, bouillon, raisins, cumin, coriander, cayenne, and cilantro. Cover and simmer for 10 minutes. Stir and cook through for 10 more minutes, stirring occasionally.

2. Serve steaming hot over hot couscous.

4 SERVINGS
PER SERVING: 474 Calories • 1.8 Grams Fat • 3.4% Calories from Fat

Orzo with Vegetables and Parmesan

Orzo is the rice of pasta, and it's just about as versatile. Make sure you chop the vegetables to a uniform size for the most attractive presentation.

1½ cups orzo
1 cup sun-dried tomatoes
3 stalks celery, diced
1 medium red pepper, diced

½ small onion, chopped
1 tablespoon minced fresh oregano
1 tablespoon minced fresh parsley
2 tablespoons grated Parmesan cheese

1. Heat a pot of water for the pasta. Soak the sun-dried tomatoes in ⅔ cup of hot water for 10 minutes, or until soft. Reserve the soaking water and chop the tomatoes.

2. Place the soaking water from the tomatoes in a nonstick skillet and sauté the celery, red pepper, and onion for 10 minutes, or until soft.

3. Boil the orzo for 10 minutes, or until al dente. Drain.

4. In a heated bowl, mix the orzo, vegetable mixture, oregano, and parsley. Sprinkle with Parmesan and serve hot.

4 SERVINGS
PER SERVING: 178 Calories • 1.8 Grams Fat • 8.8% Calories from Fat

Eight-Vegetable Lasagna

This idea comes from Jeanne Lemlin, a fabulous cookbook author and next-town-over neighbor. Her version is "high test," but the idea of not precooking the noodles is brilliant. Thank you, Jeanne!

1 can (28 ounces) tomato puree
1 cup red wine
1 cup water
1 medium onion, chopped
3 garlic cloves, minced
½ cup chopped parsley
2 tablespoons minced fresh oregano
or 1 tablespoon dried
2 tablespoons minced fresh basil
or 2 teaspoons dried
2 egg whites (or 4 teaspoons dried
egg whites plus ¼ cup water)

1 cup nonfat ricotta cheese
½ sweet green pepper, chopped
½ sweet red pepper, chopped
1 small zucchini, chopped
1 medium carrot, shredded
10 ounces mushrooms, sliced
1 medium tomato, sliced
1 pound lasagna noodles, uncooked
1 pound nonfat mozzarella
cheese, grated
½ cup grated Parmesan cheese

1. Preheat the oven to 350°F.

2. In a large bowl, mix the tomato puree, wine, water, onion, garlic, parsley, oregano, and basil. In a separate bowl, combine the ricotta and egg whites (or pasteurized dried egg whites and water) and mix well. In a third bowl, combine the peppers, zucchini, carrot, mushrooms, and tomato.

3. Ladle 2 cups of the tomato sauce on the bottom of a 9 by 13-inch baking dish. Alternate layers of uncooked noodles, sauce, ricotta mixture, vegetables, and the mozzarella, until you have three layers, ending with the mozzarella. The lasagna should not reach the top of the pan: The noodles will need room to expand.

4. Cover the pan with aluminum foil and seal tightly (the steam generated inside will cook the noodles.) Bake for 1 hour. Remove the foil, sprinkle with Parmesan and continue baking for 15 minutes, or until the noodles are soft. Let the lasagna sit for 10 minutes before serving.

8 SERVINGS
PER SERVING: 440 Calories • 3.0 Grams Fat • 6.4% Calories from Fat

Hutspot

This is a low-fat version of a dish that figures prominently in Dutch history. When the town of Leiden was beseiged in 1574 during the war for independence from Spain, the citizens were dying of disease and starvation. Their national hero, the Prince of Orange, had his men break through a few strategic dikes, which started to flood the fields surrounding the walled-in city. The Spanish soldiers holding the town hostage had never learned to swim, and when they saw the rising water, they panicked and fled. The scout who was sent to confirm the report that the soldiers had abruptly retreated came upon a deserted campsite, where a pot containing dinner—hutspot—was still hanging over the fire. He brought the pot back as proof of their sudden liberation.

4 medium potatoes
3 medium carrots
2 medium onions
Salt and freshly ground black pepper
1 pound soy meat substitute

1. Peel the potatoes, carrots, and onions and slice them into 1-inch pieces. Put the vegetables on a steamer basket and place in a saucepan with 1 inch of water. Steam the vegetables for about 20 minutes, or until they're very soft when pierced with a knife.

2. Place the vegetables in a large mixing bowl and mash them with a potato masher. Add salt and lots of pepper to taste.

3. Heat a nonstick skillet for 20 seconds and brown the soy meat substitute. Arrange the meat substitute on top of the mashed vegetables and serve piping hot.

4 SERVINGS
PER SERVING: 243 Calories • 0.2 Gram Fat • 0.9% Calories from Fat

Excellentils

This stew was named by one of my testers. I was going to give it a homely name such as "End o' the Month Stew," since it originated at the end of the month when I was out of cash. All I had left were some rice and lentils in the cupboard and one tired carrot and some pale celery stalks in the vegetable bin. This stew was the triumphant and delicious victory of inventiveness over reality. Serve it with crusty bread.

4 cups water
½ cup brown rice
1 cup lentils
1 medium onion, chopped
2 stalks celery, chopped
1 medium carrot, chopped
½ package (5 ounces) frozen spinach
2 garlic cloves, minced
1 teaspoon cider vinegar
1 teaspoon dried basil
1 teaspoon dried sage
½ teaspoon salt
Freshly ground black pepper
2 tablespoons grated Parmesan cheese

1. Heat the water in a medium-size saucepan. Add the ingredients (except for cheese) in the order listed and mix thoroughly. Continue cooking until the mixture reaches a boil, then reduce the heat, cover, and simmer for 40 minutes, stirring occasionally.

2. Uncover and simmer for another 10 minutes, stirring so that the stew won't scorch on the bottom. Serve hot in deep bowls. Sprinkle Parmesan on top.

6 SERVINGS
PER SERVING: 192 Calories • 1.4 Grams Fat • 6.3% Calories from Fat

Cranberry Bean Chili

The contrast of the light cranberry beans and the dark kidney beans makes this chili more interesting to look at than most. For a hearty dinner serve with Zucchini Parmesan Jalapeño Bread (page 51), and a green salad. Note: Wear rubber gloves while mincing the jalapeño to protect your skin from the irritating oils.

1 can (15 ounces) cranberry beans
8 ounces red kidney beans, canned
1 medium onion, chopped
2 garlic cloves, minced
$\frac{1}{2}$ sweet red pepper, chopped
1 medium jalapeño pepper, minced
1 can (28 ounces) tomatoes, undrained
1 teaspoon ground cumin
1 teaspoon dried oregano
$\frac{1}{4}$ teaspoon hot sauce
Salt
1 tablespoon grated Parmesan cheese
$\frac{1}{4}$ cup freshly ground cilantro

1. Combine both kinds of beans, the onion, garlic, red pepper, jalapeño, tomatoes, cumin, oregano, and hot sauce in a saucepan and simmer for 30 minutes. Add salt to taste if necessary and more hot sauce to taste.

2. Serve in a deep bowl, sprinkled with Parmesan and cilantro.

4 SERVINGS
PER SERVING: 205 Calories • 1.7 Grams Fat • 7.0% Calories from Fat

Pasta e Fagioli

This hearty meal can be prepared and cooked in less than 30 minutes, and is bursting with minerals and vitamins. Serve with a warm baguette.

1 medium onion, chopped
2 garlic cloves, minced
1 medium sweet red pepper, chopped
$\frac{2}{3}$ cup tomato juice
1$\frac{1}{2}$ packages (15 ounces) spinach, frozen
1 can (15$\frac{1}{2}$ ounces) small white beans, drained
1 cup canned tomatoes, drained
Freshly ground black pepper
6 cups cooked macaroni
2 tablespoons grated Parmesan cheese

1. In a large saucepan, combine the onion, garlic, red pepper, and tomato juice. Let the vegetables simmer over medium heat for 5 minutes.
2. Add the spinach, cover, and let the mixture heat through for 5 minutes.
3. Add the beans and tomatoes. Break up the tomatoes with the end of a wooden spoon and let the mixture simmer for another 10 minutes. Add pepper to taste.
4. Serve very hot over macaroni in deep bowls and sprinkle with Parmesan.

4 SERVINGS
PER SERVING: 522 Calories • 3.4 Grams Fat • 5.8% Calories from Fat

Focaccia Dough

Focaccia dough is the basis for many, many combinations of foods, much like pizza. A few of them follow, but dream up your own variations.

1 cup water
1 teaspoon sugar
1 envelope active dry yeast
2 cups plus 1 tablespoon all-purpose flour
$\frac{1}{3}$ cup whole-wheat flour
$\frac{3}{4}$ teaspoon salt

1. The cup of water used for this purpose must be lukewarm (105°–115°F). (Colder, and the yeast won't activate; warmer, and the yeast will die.) Pour the water and sugar into a bowl and sprinkle the yeast over the top. Let it sit for 10 minutes.
2. Place the flours (less the 1 tablespoon) and salt in a food processor bowl and using a plastic blade, mix well. As the blade is turning, add the yeast mixture. Let the processor run 1 minute, or until the dough forms a ball.
3. If you're mixing by hand, combine the flours and salt in a large bowl. Add the yeast mixture and using a wooden spoon and your hands, mix until it sticks together in a ball. Turn the dough out onto a work surface that has been sprinkled with some flour and knead for 4 minutes. Form the dough into a ball.
4. Spray a large bowl with cooking spray and place the dough in the bowl. Cover the bowl with a damp towel and let the dough rise for 1 hour in a warm, draft-free place. It will double in volume.
5. Coat a nonstick baking sheet with cooking spray.
6. Punch down the dough and sprinkle with 1 tablespoon of flour. Take it out of the bowl and knead for 30 seconds, incorporating the flour to make the surface less sticky. Place the dough on the baking sheet and, using your fingertips, push it out to make a 10-inch circle. Cover the dough with a damp towel and let it rise for 30 minutes in a warm, draft-free place.
7. Meanwhile, prepare a topping and preheat the oven to 425°F.
8. Uncover the dough and, with your fingertips, gently push it down all over. (The surface will look dimpled.) Cover it with the topping of your choice and bake for 20 to 25 minutes, or until it's nicely browned. Serve immediately.

4 SERVINGS
PER SERVING: 281 Calories • 1.0 Gram Fat • 3.1% Calories from Fat

Caponata Focaccia

I love caponata, so I was looking for an other way to eat it—and this was it!

1 focaccia dough (page 105)
2 cups caponata (page 12)
1 tablespoon grated Parmesan cheese

1. Prepare the focaccia dough.
2. Prepare the caponata.
3. Preheat the oven to 425°F. When the dough is ready to bake, spread with the caponata. Sprinkle with Parmesan and bake for 20 to 25 minutes, or until the crust is nicely browned. Serve hot.

4 SERVINGS
PER SERVING: 361 Calories • 1.8 Grams Fat • 4.4% Calories from Fat

Sun-Dried Tomato and Onion Focaccia

Sun-dried tomato sauce gives a deep red color and intense tomato flavor to focaccia.

1 focaccia dough (page 105)
2 ounces sun-dried tomatoes, dry packed
1⅓ cups nonfat vegetable or chicken broth
1 small onion, minced
2 garlic cloves, minced
1 tablespoon minced fresh oregano (or 1 teaspoon dried)

1. Prepare the focaccia dough.
2. Combine the tomatoes and broth in a saucepan. Simmer for 15 minutes. Cool slightly. Place the tomatoes and the broth in a food processor or blender and process until smooth. Set aside.
3. Coat a nonstick skillet with cooking spray. Add the onions and brown for 3 minutes. Add the garlic and oregano and brown one more minute. Combine the onion mixture with the tomatoes and mix.
4. Preheat the oven to 425°F. Spread the tomato sauce over the dough. Sprinkle the cheese over all. Place the dough in the oven and bake for 20 to 25 minutes. Serve immediately.

4 SERVINGS
PER SERVING: 333 Calories • 1.5 Grams Fat • 3.9% Calories from Fat

Roasted Red Pepper Focaccia

Now that I've learned how easy it is to roast peppers, I make extra batches of them every time they go on sale. Here's a great way to use them.

1 focaccia dough (page 105)
2 sweet red peppers, roasted (page 29)
½ teaspoon balsamic vinegar

½ teaspoon dried basil
2 tablespoons grated
Parmesan cheese

1. Prepare the focaccia dough.
2. Preheat the oven to 425°F.
3. Skin the roasted peppers, cut in half, core, and remove the seeds. Slice the peppers into strips and combine in a bowl with the vinegar and basil.
4. Arrange the peppers on the focaccia dough and sprinkle with Parmesan. Bake for 20 to 25 minutes, or until the dough is nicely browned. Serve immediately.

4 SERVINGS
PER SERVING: 303 Calories • 1.8 Grams Fat • 5.3% Calories from Fat

Onion Focaccia

It doesn't get more rustic than this—just plain ol' onion and cheese. Makes a great dinner with a bowl of soup, but we enjoy it best late at night after a long day of work.

1 focaccia dough (page 105)
1 large onion
1 teaspoon dried oregano

Freshly ground black pepper
1 tablespoon grated Parmesan cheese

1. Prepare the focaccia dough.
2. Slice the onion and cut the slices in half.
3. Coat a nonstick skillet with cooking spray. Heat the pan for 30 seconds and add the onions. Sauté them until they are translucent. Sprinkle oregano and pepper to taste over all.
4. Preheat the oven to 425°F.
5. Cover the focaccia dough with the onions and sprinkle the cheese on top. Bake for 15 to 20 minutes, or until the dough is nicely browned. Serve immediately.

4 SERVINGS
PER SERVING: 295 Calories • 1.4 Grams Fat • 4.3% Calories from Fat

Tomato Basil Pizza

Plum tomatoes are less juicy than regular tomatoes, but if regular tomatoes are more flavorful, remove some of the seeds and use them. For all of the following pizza recipes, you can make your own pizza dough if you prefer, but frozen pizza dough works just as well.

1 frozen pizza dough
1 cup nonfat ricotta cheese
1½ teaspoons minced fresh basil
(or ½ teaspoon dried)
¼ teaspoon salt
4 slices red onion
2 plum tomatoes, sliced
3 teaspoons grated Parmesan cheese
3 fresh basil leaves
Freshly ground black pepper

1. Preheat the oven to 475°F. Mix the ricotta, basil, and salt in a medium-size bowl. Dollop it on the dough and spread. Arrange the onion slices on top of the ricotta and the tomato slices over that. Sprinkle with Parmesan cheese.

2. Bake for 10 minutes, or until the crust is nicely browned. Meanwhile, tightly roll the basil leaves and slice thinly. Remove the pizza from the oven, grind pepper to taste over it, and sprinkle with the basil. Serve immediately.

6 SLICES
PER SERVING: 208 Calories • 2.0 Grams Fat • 8.5% Calories from Fat

Mexican Pizza

I know this title mixes cuisines, but if you just think of pizza crust as a great bottom, you can put anything on top. Hey, this is America, right?

1 frozen pizza dough
3 plum tomatoes, diced
2 scallions, minced
1 jalapeño pepper, minced

2 tablespoons fresh cilantro, minced
¼ cup nonfat ricotta cheese
Pinch of cayenne

1. Prepare the pizza dough according to the package directions.

2. Preheat the oven to 425°F. Coat a nonstick baking sheet with cooking spray.

3. In a small bowl, mix the tomatoes, scallions, jalapeño, cilantro, and ricotta. Add cayenne to taste. Dollop it on the crust with a spoon and spread evenly.

4. Bake for 15 minutes, or until the crust is nicely browned.

6 SLICES
PER SERVING: 154 Calories • 1.7 Grams Fat • 9.9% Calories from Fat

Mushroom-Onion Pizza

If you like this mushroom-onion combination a lot, as I do, make some extra to use in a fajita the next day.

1 frozen pizza dough
2 large onions
10 ounces mushrooms
¼ cup tomato juice
2 tablespoons white wine

1 teaspoon tamari soy sauce
1 teaspoon dried oregano
1½ teaspoons minced fresh thyme
or ½ teaspoon dried

1. Prepare the pizza dough according to the package directions.

2. Preheat the oven to 425°F. In a large saucepan, combine the onions, mushrooms, tomato juice, wine, soy sauce, oregano, and thyme. Simmer for 15 minutes, or until the vegetables are soft.

3. Spread the vegetable mixture on the pizza dough. Bake for 8 to 10 minutes, or until the crust is nicely browned.

6 SLICES
PER SERVING: 157 Calories • 1.7 Grams Fat • 10.0% Calories from Fat

Spinach Pizza

A classic combination and a treat—and totally guilt-free because of the no-fat sausage-flavored soy meat substitute.

1 frozen pizza dough

1 package (10 ounces) frozen spinach

1 pound sausage-flavored soy meat substitute

1 teaspoon oregano

1 tablespoon grated Parmesan cheese

1. Prepare the pizza dough according to the package directions. Preheat the oven to 425°F.

2. Defrost the spinach and drain the liquid in a colander.

3. Coat a nonstick skillet with cooking spray. Heat for 20 seconds and add the meat substitute, breaking it up with a wooden spoon. When the "sausage" begins to brown, transfer it to a mixing bowl. Add the drained spinach and oregano. Mix well.

4. Spread the mixture over the pizza crust. Sprinkle with Parmesan. Bake for 15 to 20 minutes, or until the crust is nicely browned.

6 SLICES
PER SERVING: 238 Calories • 1.9 Grams Fat • 7.2% Calories from Fat

Tacos in Tortilla Chips

My family ranks this as one of their favorites—not just because they like the taste, but also because it's fun to make. If you can find nonfat taco shells, by all means use them, but these little guys were just fine, and perhaps even more fun.

1 can (15 ounces) black beans

½ cup tomato juice

½ teaspoon ground cumin

40 nonfat tortilla chips

1 recipe Tomato Cilantro Salsa (page 9)

3 cups shredded lettuce

1 cup nonfat sour cream

2 cup shredded nonfat cheddar cheese

1. In a nonstick skillet, heat the black beans, tomato juice, and cumin. Simmer until most of the juice is absorbed.

2. Place the chips in a basket. Put the salsa, lettuce, sour cream, and beans in separate bowls. Pile spoonfuls of the various ingredients over the chips for each serving.

4 SERVINGS
PER SERVING: 292 Calories • 1.8 Grams Fat • 4.2% Calories from Fat

ENTRÉES

Spaghetti and Pseudo Meatballs in Tomato Sauce

Serve these over a mountain of spaghetti and your guests will never know they're eating a vegetarian meal. For additional flavor, substitute half the beef-flavored meat replacement with the sausage-flavored kind.

7 ounces beef-flavored soy meat substitute
$\frac{1}{4}$ cup bread crumbs, seasoned
1 teaspoon Dijon mustard
$\frac{1}{2}$ teaspoon oregano
$\frac{1}{2}$ teaspoon paprika
$\frac{1}{4}$ teaspoon olive oil
3 cups tomato puree
1 cup sweet chopped green pepper
1 cup chopped onion
1 tablespoon minced fresh oregano (or 1 teaspoon dried)
$\frac{1}{2}$ teaspoon salt
1 pound spaghetti
2 tablespoons grated Parmesan cheese

1. In a medium-size bowl, combine the meat substitute, crumbs, mustard, oregano, and paprika. Mix well. Form into 12 walnut-size balls.

2. Rub the oil over the bottom of a nonstick skillet and heat for 1 minute. Add the meatballs and sauté over medium heat for 10 minutes, turning frequently to brown all sides.

3. Meanwhile, combine the tomato puree, pepper, onion, oregano, and salt in a large saucepan and simmer for 20 minutes.

4. When the meatballs are brown, add them to the tomato sauce and simmer on low heat for 10 minutes. Heat a large pot of water for the pasta and cook according to package directions. Drain. Spoon the sauce over the pasta and sprinkle with the cheese.

4 SERVINGS
PER SERVING: 617 Calories • 3.5 Grams Fat • 5.0% Calories from Fat

Stuffed Cabbage

Stuffed cabbage rolls are a traditional Eastern European dish. The combination of tomatoes and cabbage makes the cabbage unexpectedly sweet. Instructions for fashioning a cabbage roll are much more complicated than the task itself: Take some time to play with the ingredients, or invent your own method!

1 cabbage
½ cup barley
1¾ cups vegetable broth
1 small onion, minced
2 garlic cloves, minced
2 stalks celery, minced
½ sweet red pepper, chopped
½ teaspoon paprika
1½ teaspoons minced fresh thyme (or ½ teaspoon dried)
¾ teaspoon chili powder
3 cups tomato puree
1 teaspoon lemon juice
Salt and freshly ground black pepper

1. Preheat the oven to 350°F. Put a large pot of water on to boil. Carefully pull 12 whole outer leaves off the cabbage, keeping the leaves intact. Reserve the rest of the cabbage.

2. Place the 12 leaves in the boiling water. Turn off the heat, cover the pot, and let the leaves stand for 5 minutes. Then drain the leaves and cut off the outside of the thick rib. Set aside.

3. Boil the barley with 1½ cups of the broth for 50 minutes, or until the barley is done. Let cool.

4. In a nonstick skillet combine the remaining broth, onion, garlic, celery, red pepper, paprika, thyme, and ¼ teaspoon of the chili powder. Simmer for 5 minutes, or until the onion becomes transparent. Add to the barley and mix well. Let cool.

5. Finely chop the remaining cabbage until you have 2 cups. Line it on the bottom of an ovenproof casserole dish. In a mixing bowl, combine the tomato puree with the remaining ½ teaspoon of chili powder plus salt and pepper to taste. Spoon 2 cups of the tomato sauce over the chopped cabbage.

6. Place a cabbage leaf on a cutting board, rib side toward you. Place one-twelfth of the barley stuffing in the center of the leaf. Fold the bottom part of the leaf over the stuffing. Then fold in the sides. Roll the leaf until you have a little package. Secure it with a toothpick if you like. Place the cabbage roll, seam-side down, in the casserole dish. Repeat with the remaining leaves and stuffing.

7. Pour the remaining 2 cups of tomato sauce over the stuffed cabbage rolls and cover the casserole dish with aluminum foil, crimping the edges tightly. Bake for 1 hour, checking near the end so that the casserole doesn't dry out. Add a bit of water if it does.

6 SERVINGS
PER SERVING: 150 Calories • 0.8 Gram Fat • 4.1% Calories from Fat

Polenta with Eggplant Tomato Sauce

The idea to put a bit of jalepeño pepper into the polenta came from Elizabeth's Restaurant in Pittsfield, Massachusetts. This is my pared-down version of their delicious dish.

$\frac{1}{2}$ medium eggplant, chopped
1 cup canned tomatoes, diced
1 medium onion, chopped
1 garlic clove, minced
1 teaspoon oregano
1 teaspoon dried basil
$\frac{1}{2}$ cup nonfat plain yogurt
Salt and freshly ground black pepper
1$\frac{1}{4}$ cups instant polenta
2 teaspoons minced jalapeño
$\frac{1}{2}$ teaspoon freshly ground black pepper
$\frac{1}{4}$ cup chopped fresh cilantro
$\frac{1}{4}$ cup grated Parmesan cheese

1. Place the eggplant, tomatoes, onion, garlic, oregano, and basil in a saucepan and simmer for 45 minutes. Add the yogurt and heat through. Add salt and pepper to taste.
2. Follow the package directions for the polenta. During the last minute of cooking, add the jalapeño pepper, black pepper, and cheese. Add salt to taste.
3. Serve the polenta on heated plates, pour the sauce over, and sprinkle with the cilantro and Parmesan.

4 SERVINGS
PER SERVING: 325 Calories • 2.5 Grams Fat • 6.8% Calories from Fat

Polenta with Mushrooms

The mushrooms give this dish a woodsy, hearty flavor. If you can't serve it immediately, spread the polenta in an pan and reheat in an oven or "fry" it up in a nonstick skillet coated with cooking spray.

1 large portabella mushroom
5 ounces mushrooms
1 teaspoon minced fresh oregano
Salt and freshly ground black pepper
13 ounces instant polenta
2 tablespoons grated Parmesan cheese

1. Coat a nonstick skillet with cooking spray and place over medium heat. Add the mushrooms and stir constantly until they start to release their moisture. Cook until the mushrooms are wilted and soft. Remove from heat. Add the oregano and salt and pepper to taste. Set aside.

2. Cook the polenta according to package directions, adding salt to taste.

3. When the polenta is done, add the mushrooms and mix well. Sprinkle with the Parmesan and serve immediately.

5 SERVINGS
PER SERVING: 263 Calories • 1.2 Grams Fat • 4.3% Calories from Fat

Potato and Pea Curry

This recipe lends itself well to using up leftovers. Try mixing in steamed carrots, cauliflower, or green peppers as well. Serve with basmati rice topped with a dollop of plain yogurt.

1 medium onion, chopped	1 teaspoon ground cumin
2 garlic cloves, minced	$\frac{1}{4}$ teaspoon ground coriander
1 cup tomato puree	$\frac{1}{2}$ teaspoon grated ginger
1 cup water	$\frac{1}{4}$ teaspoon cayenne
1 teaspoon apple-cider vinegar	4 large potatoes
1 teaspoon curry powder	2 cups frozen peas
1 teaspoon ground turmeric	

1. In a large saucepan, combine the onion, garlic, tomato puree, water, vinegar, and spices. Simmer for 20 minutes. Cut the potatoes into 1-inch cubes and steam until tender.

2. When the sauce is done, add the peas and bring back to a simmer. Carefully add the potatoes and heat through, stirring occasionally.

4 SERVINGS
PER SERVING: 163 Calories • 0.7 Gram Fat • 3.8% Calories from Fat

Soba Noodles

The first time I ate soba noodles, it was clear to me that this must be comfort food for the Japanese. Nourishing and filling, it's a great vegetarian counterpart to chicken soup.

1 pound soba noodles	2 carrots sliced
3 cups chopped fresh spinach	2 scallions, minced
$1\frac{1}{2}$ cups snow peas	3 tablespoons sweet miso
2 cups water	

1. Cook the soba noodles in a large pot of boiling water for 6 or 7 minutes, or until cooked al dente. Rinse immediately under cold water and set aside.

2. Clean the spinach under running water to remove any grit. Chop the spinach and diagonally cut each snow pea into 3 pieces.

3. Bring the water to a boil. Add the carrots and simmer for 10 minutes, or until they soften. Add the scallions, spinach, and snow peas. Cook for 3 minutes more.

4. Add the soba noodles and heat through. Stir in the miso. Serve hot in deep bowls.

4 SERVINGS
PER SERVING: 455 Calories • 1.9 Grams Fat • 3.5% Calories from Fat

Roasted Vegetable Heroes

Vegetable Heroes are a great way to meet your vegetable quota on a night when you have little time. I first tasted roasted vegetable sandwiches during a vacation to the Napa Sonoma countryside, where the vegetables were bursting with flavor and the wine flowed freely. Use additional chopped fresh herbs to flavor the mayonnaise if you like.

1 baguette	$\frac{1}{2}$ medium red onion
$\frac{1}{4}$ cup nonfat mayonnaise	1 teaspoon minced fresh oregano
2 teaspoons mustard	Salt and freshly ground black pepper
1 medium eggplant	4 garlic cloves
1 medium sweet red pepper	2 teaspoons minced fresh parsley
2 medium tomatoes	Pinch of chili powder

1. Preheat the oven to 350°F. Line 2 nonstick baking sheets with parchment paper.

2. Slice the baguette lengthwise. In a small bowl combine the mayonnaise and mustard and mix well. Spread the mayonnaise mixture on each side of the baguette. Set aside.

3. Slice the eggplant into rounds no thicker than ¼-inch thick. Remove the stem and seeds from the pepper and cut into strips. Slice the tomato and onion into ¼-inch thick rounds. Place the vegetables on the lined baking sheets and sprinkle with the oregano and salt and pepper to taste. Place the whole garlic cloves in their papery skins on the sheet between the vegetables. Bake for 30 minutes, or until the vegetables are soft.

4. Remove the vegetables from the oven. Place between the two halves of the prepared baguette and sprinkle with parsley. Cut into four pieces and serve warm.

4 SERVINGS
PER SERVING: 378 Calories • 4.0 Grams Fat • 9.4% Calories from Fat

Fenway Subs

The inspiration for these subs came from the ones I got outside Fenway Park before ball games. Theirs are definitely not low-fat treats. But when you're trying to cut down on fat intake, the memories of those subs might haunt you as they do me. So here it is: Dig in and play ball!

14 ounces sausage-flavored soy meat substitute
2 medium sweet red peppers
2 medium sweet green peppers
3 medium onions
$\frac{1}{2}$ cup vegetable broth or nonfat beef broth
1 teaspoon mustard
$\frac{1}{2}$ teaspoon vinegar
4 8-inch submarine sandwich rolls

1. Coat a nonstick skillet with cooking spray. Heat for 10 seconds; then add the meat substitute. Stir as it browns. Remove the "meat" from the skillet and set aside.

2. Add the peppers, onions, broth, mustard, and vinegar to the same skillet. Simmer for 5 minutes. Return the "meat" to the skillet and heat through.

3. Slice the buns lengthwise and pile on the filling. Serve hot.

4 SERVINGS
PER SERVING: 324 Calories • 1.3 Grams Fat • 3.4% Calories from Fat

Bean Burgers Deluxe

These "burgers" are fast to make and a perfect mate to warm soup. You can vary the beans and spices. Use rubber gloves while preparing the jalapeño pepper to protect your skin from irritating oils.

½ jalapeño pepper
⅓ cup tomato juice
1 small onion, minced
1 garlic clove, minced
¼ teaspoon ground cumin
½ cup crushed matzo crackers
2 egg whites (or 4 teaspoons pasteurized dried egg whites
plus ¼ cup water)
1 teaspoon lemon juice
¼ cup minced fresh cilantro
1 teaspoon minced fresh oregano
1 can (15 ounces) pinto beans, drained
4 hamburger buns
1 tablespoon nonfat mayonnaise
4 tomato slices
1 teaspoon grated Parmesan cheese
1 tablespoon ketchup

1. Line a nonstick pan with parchment paper. Preheat the oven to 350°F.

2. Cut the jalepeño in half, remove the seeds and white fibers, and mince.

3. In a small nonstick skillet, combine the tomato juice, onion, garlic, cumin, and jalapeño. Simmer for 5 minutes, or until the onion is soft.

4. In a food processor, process the matzo crackers, egg whites, and lemon juice, scraping down occasionally, for 30 seconds. Add the tomato-juice mixture, and process for 30 seconds more. Add the cilantro, oregano, and pinto beans, and process until well incorporated but not totally smooth.

5. Spoon 4 equal portions of the mixture on the parchment and flatten them out to the shape and size of a burger. Bake for 25 minutes. Slice the buns in half and spread the mayonnaise over the bottom halves. Place the burgers on the buns, top with a tomato slice, and sprinkle with Parmesan cheese. Spread ketchup on the inside of the top bun and cover.

4 SERVINGS
PER SERVING: 383 Calories • 3.7 Grams Fat • 8.5% Calories from Fat

CHAPTER 4

SIDE DISHES

Nowhere does low-fat cooking shine brighter than with grains and vegetables. Blessedly low in fat, vegetables and grains vary in texture, color, and flavor, running the gamut from sweet to bitter, bland to spicy, crunchy to mushy. They offer something for every palate.

It's what we often do to our grains and vegetables that lands us in trouble in the fat department: adding dairy toppings, sauces, and cheeses that are filled with fat. The challenge is to combine flavors and textures that allow us variety while avoiding these and other fats.

One strategy is to eat produce in season, when it's naturally bursting with flavor and needs little doctoring. Compare in your imagination the pink, hard, rubber-ball midwinter tomato from the supermarket to the soft, deep-red, fragrant August tomato at the farmers' market—the former will need help if it's ever to be considered food while the latter is perfect just as it is. In-season produce is also easier on the pocketbook.

The herbs and spices of various ethnic cuisines are great inspiration for novel flavors. However, these foods are rarely low in fat. When food was meant to support hard physical labor, it was necessary to raise the caloric content with added fats.

The side-dish recipes that follow are meant to be a springboard for your own inventiveness and imagination. Look at the strategies employed in the recipes and see how you can adapt them. Purees can be made with different combinations of root vegetables and squashes, beans can be substituted for one another, and an alternate green leafy vegetable can take the place of the one listed.

RICE AND GRAINS

Pastas, rice, and grains are perfectly suited to the low-fat life, since most are either low in fat or contain no fat at all. Gone are the days when starches were considered fattening and avoided by the weight-conscious. But remember, low in fat doesn't mean low in calories. So eat these wonderful foods by all means—but don't overdo it!

Kasha with Leeks

Kasha, also known as buckwheat groats, is a typical Eastern European food, hearty and filling. Customarily it's accompanied by various fats during cooking. This version with leeks and mushrooms brings out the best of this grain in a healthful way.

1 egg white (or 2 teaspoons pasteurized dried egg whites
plus 2 tablespoons water)
1 cup buckwheat groats
3 cups water
5 ounces mushrooms, sliced
1 cup chopped leeks
$\frac{1}{4}$ teaspoon salt
$\frac{1}{4}$ teaspoon dried sage

1. In a mixing bowl, whip the egg white until foamy. Add the groats and mix well.

2. Heat the water to boiling and have it ready. Heat a nonstick pan for 30 seconds and add the groats mixture. Stir constantly until the groats are almost dry and slightly toasted.

3. Add the boiling water and the mushrooms, leeks, salt, and sage. Simmer for 15 minutes. Fluff with a fork and serve.

4 SERVINGS
PER SERVING: 162 Calories • 1.3 Grams Fat • 6.7% Calories from Fat

Broccoli Rabe Risotto

Broccoli rabe has a distinctive slightly bitter taste that I love. It was very common in Holland when I was growing up, and I'm delighted that it's becoming widely available here. It doesn't look at all like broccoli but resembles a pesky weed with big leaves. To prepare, pull the leaves from the stalk and wash them.

2 cups water
2 cups chopped broccoli rabe
2 cups nonfat vegetable or chicken broth
$\frac{1}{4}$ cup chopped onion
$\frac{1}{4}$ cup white wine
1 cup arborio rice
$\frac{1}{4}$ cup grated Parmesan cheese

1. Place 1 cup of the water in a food processor or blender container with ½ cup of the broccoli rabe. Puree. Add handfuls of broccoli rabe to the mix, pureeing each until all the broccoli is pureed. Set aside.

2. In a small saucepan, heat the broth to boiling. In a separate saucepan, combine the onion, wine, and rice and stir over medium heat until the wine is absorbed by the rice. Stirring continuously, over low heat add ¼ cup of the hot broth to the rice until it's absorbed. In this manner, gradually add 1 cup of the hot broth, stirring after each addition.

3. Add the broccoli rabe puree to the rice in three batches, stirring after each to absorb. Then gradually add the remaining 1 cup of broth in ¼-cup increments as outlined in Step 2. Taste the rice, which should by now be very soft. The broccoli rabe will have formed a thick creamy sauce around it.

4. Add the Parmesan cheese and stir to combine. Serve on heated plates.

4 SERVINGS
PER SERVING: 205 Calories • 1.6 Grams Fat • 7.2% Calories from Fat

Double Mushroom Rice

This is a hearty, meaty rice. Experiment with different mushrooms in this dish, depending on what's available and looks fresh in the market.

12 crimini mushrooms
1 portabella mushroom
5 shallots, minced

1 small sweet red pepper, chopped
1 cup white rice
2 cups nonfat vegetable or beef broth

1. Clean all the mushrooms and cut off the stems. Slice the crimini. Cut the portabella in fourths and slice each section.
2. Preheat a nonstick skillet. Stirring continuously, add the mushrooms, shallots, and red peppers. Continue to stir until the mushrooms start to lose their moisture.
3. Slowly add the broth and mix well. Mix in the rice and bring to a boil. Reduce the heat, cover, and simmer for 20 minutes, or until the rice is done. Fluff with a fork before serving.

4 SERVINGS
PER SERVING: 217 Calories • 0.6 Gram Fat • 2.3% Calories from Fat

Herbed Rice

If you like herbed rice a lot and like to eat it frequently, consider prepackaging your own mix. Set out six bowls and measure out six portions of every ingredient except the water and garlic. Pour the measured rice and spices into plastic freezer bags, which are sturdier than storage bags, and you'll have this wonderful rice on hand at a moment's notice.

2 cups water
1 cup rice
2 garlic cloves, minced
1 teaspoon dried thyme

$\frac{3}{4}$ teaspoon dried oregano
$\frac{3}{4}$ teaspoon salt
$\frac{1}{2}$ teaspoon dried tarragon
$\frac{1}{4}$ teaspoon chili powder

1. Bring the water to a boil in a medium-size saucepan. Add the rice, garlic, thyme, oregano, salt, tarragon, and chili powder.
2. Return to a boil and stir. Reduce the heat, cover, and simmer for 20 minutes, or until the rice is done. Fluff with a fork and serve hot.

4 SERVINGS
PER SERVING: 174 Calories • 0.4 Gram Fat • 2.2% Calories from Fat

Rice with Beet Greens

This nourishing and substantial side dish can also be made with other greens such as chard. The rice in this version will take on a beautiful hue—from the red of the beet-green stems and the yellow of the turmeric—and the greens will melt into little flecks.

10 ounces beet greens	1 teaspoon ground turmeric
2 cups water	1 tablespoon vegetable-broth mix
1 medium onion, chopped	1 cup white rice
4 garlic cloves, minced	1 tablespoon tamari soy sauce

1. Wash the beet greens very thoroughly with several changes of water. Shred the leaves and chop the stems.

2. Pour the 2 cups water into a medium-size saucepan and add the greens, onion, garlic, turmeric, broth, and rice. Bring to a boil and stir. Reduce the heat, cover, and, stirring occasionally, simmer for 20 minutes, or until the rice is done.

3. Stir in the soy sauce and serve hot.

6 SERVINGS
PER SERVING: 134 Calories • 0.3 Gram Fat • 1.9% Calories from Fat

Sweet Onion Basmati Rice

This is a mild-flavored yellow rice, good with any curry-flavored dish or grilled chicken.

$2\frac{1}{2}$ cups water
$\frac{1}{2}$ medium onion, chopped
10 dates, chopped
$\frac{1}{2}$ teaspoon ground turmeric
$\frac{1}{4}$ teaspoon salt
1 cup basmati rice

1. Bring the water to a boil. Add the onion, dates, turmeric, and salt.

2. Rinse the rice under running water until the water runs clear. Add the rinsed rice to the boiling water, cover, and simmer for 20 minutes. Fluff the rice before serving.

4 SERVINGS
PER SERVING: 226 Calories • 0.4 Gram Fat • 1.4% Calories from Fat

Lemon Parsley Rice

This rice has a mild, fresh taste and would blend well with dishes that have a good sauce.

2 cups water
1 medium onion, chopped
$\frac{1}{2}$ teaspoon salt
2 pieces lemon zest

1 tablespoon lemon juice
1 cup white rice
$1\frac{1}{2}$ tablespoons snipped fresh chives
$\frac{1}{4}$ cup minced fresh parsley

1. Bring the water to a boil in a saucepan. Stir in the onion, salt, lemon zest, and lemon juice. Stir well.
2. Add the rice and bring to a boil. Reduce the heat, cover, and simmer for 20 minutes. Remove the zest.
3. Sprinkle with the chives and parsley and mix them in while fluffing the rice with a fork. Serve hot.

4 SERVINGS
PER SERVING: 187 Calories • 0.5 Gram Fat • 2.5% Calories from Fat

Wild Rice with Asparagus

This delicately flavored dish blends the subtle flavors of wild rice, basmati rice, and asparagus.

24 thin asparagus stalks
$3\frac{1}{2}$ cups nonfat vegetable or chicken broth
$\frac{1}{2}$ cup wild rice
1 cup brown basmati rice

$\frac{1}{2}$ cup chopped shallots
$\frac{1}{2}$ teaspoon salt
$\frac{1}{2}$ teaspoon ground rosemary
Salt and freshly ground black pepper

1. Snap the hard, woody ends off the asparagus and cut them into 2-inch pieces. Set aside.
2. In a medium-size saucepan, bring the broth to a boil. Stir in the wild rice, basmati rice, shallots, salt, and rosemary. Stir. Return to a boil. Reduce the heat, cover, and simmer for 50 minutes.
3. Stir the asparagus into the rice. Cover and let simmer over very low heat for 5 more minutes, or until the asparagus is crisp yet tender. Add salt and pepper to taste.

6 SERVINGS
PER SERVING: 211 Calories • 0.6 Gram Fat • 2.5% Calories from Fat

Moroccan Brown Rice

A tasty accompaniment for kabobs or other grilled foods, Moroccan Brown Rice also provides the extra nutrients of brown rice. Add heat to this dish with more cayenne.

2 cups nonfat vegetable or chicken broth
1 cup brown rice
½ teaspoon salt
½ teaspoon ground cumin
¼ teaspoon ground turmeric
¼ teaspoon ground ginger
1 cup diced carrots

1 cup diced zucchini
¼ cup minced fresh parsley
¼ cup minced fresh mint
2 tablespoons lemon juice
2 tablespoons nonfat plain yogurt
Pinch of cayenne

1. In a saucepan, bring the broth to a boil. Stir in the rice, salt, cumin, turmeric, and ginger. Bring back to a boil, reduce the heat, cover, and simmer for 35 minutes.

2. Add the carrots and simmer for 10 minutes. Add the zucchini and simmer for 5 more minutes, or until the rice is cooked.

3. Stir in the parsley, mint, lemon juice, yogurt, and cayenne. Mix well. You may serve this hot, warm, or cold. If served cold, you might want to add more salt.

4 SERVINGS
PER SERVING: 216 Calories • 1.6 Grams Fat • 6.5% Calories from Fat

Basil Orzo

Orzo is not rice but a pasta shaped like rice. With this pesto sauce it makes a wonderful side dish, but it can also be served as a salad with a bowl of minestrone.

1 cup orzo
¼ cup water
1 garlic clove
1 teaspoon low-sodium soy sauce

1 tablespoon plus 1 teaspoon grated Parmesan cheese
1 cup fresh basil, tightly packed

1. Bring a pot of water to a boil. Cook the orzo according to the package directions.

2. Meanwhile, place the water, garlic, soy sauce, and 1 tablespoon Parmesan cheese in a food processor or blender and process until the garlic is liquefied. Add the basil in batches and blend until smooth.

3. Put the drained orzo in a serving bowl and pour the basil sauce over it. Mix well. Sprinkle with the remaining Parmesan.

3 SERVINGS
PER SERVING: 118 Calories • 1.2 Grams Fat • 9.0% Calories from Fat

VEGETABLES

No foods are more suitable for low-fat cuisine than those in the vegetable family. But their low fat content is not the only reason to partake of vegetables: Many are loaded with antioxidants, as well as other beneficial nutrients. After a while you won't even miss the buttery sauces. By decreasing your fat intake, you actually sharpen your taste buds, enabling them to enjoy the taste of fresh vegetables like never before.

Artichokes with Sour Cream Dip

Artichokes always remind me of the summers we camped in the south of France. We would sit in our canvas chairs under a giant walnut tree, leisurely eating this delicious treat. You can make this sauce, or use any fat-free dressing you like for dipping.

$\frac{1}{4}$ cup nonfat sour cream
$\frac{1}{4}$ cup nonfat mayonnaise
1 teaspoon minced shallot
1 teaspoon white wine

1 teaspoon minced fresh parsley
Salt and freshly ground black pepper
4 medium artichokes

1. Whisk together the sour cream, mayonnaise, shallot, wine, parsley, and salt and pepper to taste in a medium-size mixing bowl and let the flavors blend for 1 hour.

2. Meanwhile, place a vegetable steamer in a saucepan and add water to the bottom of the basket. If the artichokes have spines at the ends of their leaves, you might want to trim them with scissors. If you do, cut a lemon in half and rub it over the cut edges to prevent discoloration.

3. Place the artichokes in the basket and steam for 30 to 45 minutes, or until an outer leaf is easily removed and a knife easily pierces the bottom.

4. Serve the artichokes, warm, hot, or cool, with the sauce. Pull off individual leaves, scoop some of the sauce onto the bottom part, and with your teeth scrape off the soft cooked portion. You'll need a bowl on the table for discarded leaves. When you've eaten all the leaves, scoop out the fuzzy center part, leaving the delicious "heart" to eat. Cut this heart into bite-size pieces and dip in the sauce.

4 SERVINGS
PER SERVING: 89 Calories • 0.2 Gram Fat • 1.9% Calories from Fat

Broccoli with Mushroom Sauce

This mushroom sauce would also do well over toast, for a guilt-free, late-night snack.

1 head broccoli
12 ounces mushrooms
4 ounces skim milk
1 tablespoon flour
1 teaspoon vegetable-broth mix

1. Place a vegetable steamer in a saucepan and add water to the bottom of the basket. Cut the broccoli into florets and steam for 7 minutes, or until they're bright green and tender-crisp.

2. Meanwhile, place 4 ounces of the mushrooms in a food processor or blender. Add the milk, flour, and broth mix and process.

3. Slice the remaining mushrooms. Heat a nonstick skillet for 30 seconds. Pour in the milk mixture and cook over medium heat, stirring constantly, until it boils. Add the sliced mushrooms and heat for 5 minutes, or until the mushrooms are soft.

4. Place the steamed broccoli in a warm bowl. Pour the sauce over the broccoli and serve.

4 SERVINGS
PER SERVING: 47 Calories • 0.5 Gram Fat • 8.2% Calories from Fat

Broccoli Rabe with Crimini Mushrooms

This recipe brings out the slightly bitter taste of broccoli rabe, but you can use it for other dark-green vegetables and a variety of mushrooms.

4 cups broccoli rabe
1 medium onion, chopped
2 garlic cloves, minced

2 cups crimini mushrooms
$\frac{1}{4}$ cup white wine
Salt and freshly ground black pepper

1. Clean the broccoli rabe in cold water, and tear the leaves from the stalks. If the leaves are large, chop them into smaller pieces.

2. Heat a nonstick skillet for 20 seconds. Add the onion and brown for 1 minute while stirring. Add the garlic and mushrooms and continue to stir until the mushrooms start to give up their liquid. Add the wine and the broccoli rabe, cover, and steam for 5 minutes. Add a little water at the end of the cooking period if the mixture gets too dry. Serve hot with salt and pepper to taste.

4 SERVINGS
PER SERVING: 36 Calories • 0.3 Gram Fat • 8.8% Calories from Fat

Brussels Sprouts

If you've not had much success warming up to brussels sprouts before, I urge you to try this simple version. I came upon it accidentally when I had a plate of brussels sprouts before me and was struck by a sudden urge to have tamari sauce. The combination of vegetable and condiment from opposite sides of the globe seemed odd, but one bite took away all doubt: They are made for each other.

$\frac{3}{4}$ pound brussels sprouts
2 tablespoons tamari soy sauce

1. Place a vegetable steamer in a saucepan and add water to the bottom of the basket. Cut the brussels sprouts in halves or quarters and steam them until they're soft when pierced with a fork. Steaming time will vary considerably depending on the size of the sprouts, but don't overcook them.

2. Place the brussels sprouts in a serving bowl and sprinkle the soy sauce liberally over them. Serve immediately.

4 SERVINGS
PER SERVING: 37 Calories • 0.2 Gram Fat • 4.8% Calories from Fat

Red Cabbage and Apples

This sweetly spiced, beautifully colored dish goes well with boiled potatoes and plain grilled chicken.

$\frac{1}{2}$ small red cabbage, sliced
2 small apples, chopped
$\frac{1}{4}$ cup water
$\frac{1}{2}$ teaspoon apple-cider vinegar
$\frac{1}{4}$ teaspoon ground cloves
$\frac{1}{8}$ teaspoon salt

1. Place all the ingredients in a medium-size saucepan and bring the water to a boil.

2. Reduce the heat, cover, and simmer for 20 minutes, stirring occasionally. Serve hot or warm.

4 SERVINGS
PER SERVING: 63 Calories • 0.5 Gram Fat • 6.2% Calories from Fat

Snow Peas and Carrots

A far cry from cubed frozen carrots and hard, tasteless green peas, this dish will have you remembering why that combination was such a good idea to begin with.

$\frac{1}{2}$ pound snow peas
2 carrots
$\frac{1}{3}$ cup nonfat chicken broth

1. Pull the strings off the snow peas and cut the peas on the diagonal. Peel the carrots and slice them very thin with a hand slicer.

2. Combine the broth, carrots, and peas in a saucepan and simmer for 4 minutes, or until the vegetables are soft. Serve immediately.

4 SERVINGS
PER SERVING: 39 Calories • 0.2 Gram Fat • 4.3% Calories from Fat

Carrots with Creamy Horseradish Sauce

Prepared horseradish is often colored red with beet juice, and if you use that kind you'll get a very rosy sauce that, depending on your aesthetic sensibility, looks either interesting or odd on the orange carrots. But you can also find natural beige-colored horseradish that will give the sauce a less startling color.

4 small carrots, sliced
$\frac{1}{3}$ cup nonfat sour cream
1 teaspoon minced shallots

1 teaspoon horseradish
1 teaspoon snipped fresh dill
$\frac{1}{8}$ teaspoon salt

1. Place a vegetable steamer in a medium-size saucepan and add water to the bottom of the basket. Steam the carrots for about 5 minutes, or until they're tender when pierced with a fork. (Steaming time will vary considerably depending on how old the carrots are and how thickly you slice them.)

2. In a small mixing bowl, combine the sour cream, shallots, horseradish, dill, and salt.

3. When the carrots are cooked, place them in a serving bowl and pour the sauce over them. Serve immediately.

4 SERVINGS
PER SERVING: 49 Calories • 0.1 Gram Fat • 2.6% Calories from Fat

Cauliflower with Fennel Seeds

This is a fast and easy side dish to serve with an Indian meal. Don't be afraid of the spices; they're quite wonderful in the cauliflower.

4 cups cauliflower florets
$\frac{1}{2}$ teaspoon fennel seeds

$\frac{1}{2}$ teaspoon allspice
2 teaspoons low-sodium soy sauce

1. Separate the cauliflower into florets and steam or boil them until tender, about 15 minutes.

2. In a spice grinder, grind together the fennel and allspice.

3. Heat a nonstick pan for 20 seconds and add the steamed cauliflower. Stir while the cauliflower slightly browns. Sprinkle the ground spices evenly over the cauliflower and heat 1 to 2 minutes longer.

4. Place the spiced cauliflower in a heated bowl and sprinkle it with the low-sodium soy sauce. Serve hot.

4 SERVINGS
PER SERVING: 13 Calories • 0.1 Gram Fat • 8.3% Calories from Fat

Chard Puree with Garlic and Ginger

This is inspired by an Indian dish, and it's an unusual way to eat this great vegetable.
If you like your food spicy and hot, increase the cayenne powder.

1 pound chard
½ cup water
3 garlic cloves, minced

1 teaspoon grated ginger
⅛ teaspoon cayenne
¼ teaspoon low-sodium soy sauce

1. Wash the chard and cut into 2-inch sections. In a large pot, bring the water to a boil. Add the chard, garlic, ginger and cayenne and return to a boil. Reduce the heat, cover, and simmer for 30 minutes.

2. Drain the chard. Using a food processor or blender, puree the chard until smooth. Serve piping hot. If the rest of the meal isn't yet ready, place the chard puree in a covered ovenproof bowl and keep warm in a 300°F oven until ready to serve.

4 SERVINGS
PER SERVING: 24 Calories • 0.3 Gram Fat • 7.8% Calories from Fat

Cucumber Raita

More a side dish than a real salad, this is meant to cool some of the heat from curry—
but instead, I've given it some cayenne to liven it up. If you do serve it as a cooling
condiment, omit the cayenne.

½ cup nonfat plain yogurt
¾ tablespoon minced fresh mint (or 1 teaspoon dried)
1 teaspoon lemon juice
¼ teaspoon ground cumin
Pinch of cayenne
½ medium cucumber, peeled and diced
Salt

1. Place the yogurt in a medium mixing bowl and whisk until smooth. Stir in the mint, lemon juice, cumin, and cayenne. Whisk again.

2. Add the cucumber and combine well. Add salt to taste. Refrigerate. Serve ice cold.

4 SERVINGS
PER SERVING: 21 Calories • 0.1 Gram Fat • 5.2% Calories from Fat

Watercress and Lima Beans

Watercress gets a new lease on life as a cooked vegetable. Try this dish with some warm, crusty bread spread with Vegetable Yogurt Cheese (page 9).

8 large mushrooms, sliced
$\frac{1}{2}$ cup nonfat chicken broth
$\frac{1}{4}$ teaspoon dried thyme
1 cup cooked baby lima beans, drained
3 cups chopped watercress
Salt and freshly ground black pepper

1. Place the mushrooms, broth, and thyme in a skillet and simmer over medium heat until the mushrooms are soft.
2. Stir in the lima beans and heat through. Place the watercress over the beans but do not stir in. Cover and continue to simmer until the watercress is thoroughly wilted.
3. Mix the watercress into the beans and mushrooms, grind pepper on top, and serve immediately, adding salt to taste.

4 SERVINGS
PER SERVING: 79 Calories • 0.7 Gram Fat • 7.3% Calories from Fat

Lima Beans in Sour Cream Tomato Sauce

The velvety soft taste of lima beans is sweetly accented with this rosy sauce.

1 package (10 ounces) frozen lima beans
$\frac{1}{3}$ cup nonfat sour cream
1 tablespoon tomato puree
$\frac{1}{2}$ teaspoon minced fresh thyme
4 drops Tabasco sauce
Freshly ground black pepper

1. Cook the lima beans according to package directions.
2. In a serving bowl, combine the sour cream, puree, thyme, and Tabasco. Add the hot lima beans, stir, add pepper to taste, and serve immediately.

4 SERVINGS
PER SERVING: 115 Calories • 0.3 Gram Fat • 2.5% Calories from Fat

Green Beans in Shallot Garlic Broth

Some people like their green beans crisp and some must have them buttery soft, so adjust the cooking time to your preference.

¾ pound green beans
¼ cup nonfat chicken broth
2 garlic cloves, minced
¼ cup minced shallots
¼ teaspoon salt
Freshly ground black pepper

1. Wash the green beans and cut off the ends.

2. Heat the chicken broth in a nonstick skillet. Add the garlic and shallots and place the beans on top of them. Reduce the heat, cover, and simmer for 15 minutes, or until the green beans are cooked the way you like them. Serve hot with freshly ground pepper on top.

4 SERVINGS
PER SERVING: 32 Calories • 0.1 Gram Fat • 2.5% Calories from Fat

Greek Green Beans and Tomatoes

These green beans go well with Garlic Parmesan Mashed Potatoes (page 144), which can help soak up the broth.

$\frac{3}{4}$ pound green beans
1 cup water
2 plum tomatoes, chopped
2 tablespoons plus 2 teaspoons minced fresh parsley
1 teaspoon vegetable-broth mix
$\frac{1}{2}$ teaspoon dried oregano
$\frac{1}{4}$ teaspoon balsamic vinegar
$\frac{1}{4}$ teaspoon salt
Freshly ground black pepper

1. Snap the ends off the green beans and slice the beans on the diagonal. Place the green beans with the water, tomatoes, 2 teaspoons of the parsley, the broth mix, oregano, vinegar, and salt in a medium saucepan and bring to a boil.

2. Reduce the heat and simmmer for 15 minutes. Add pepper to taste. Serve hot with the remaining 2 tablespoons of parsley sprinkled on top.

4 SERVINGS
PER SERVING: 40 Calories • 0.3 Gram Fat • 6.1% Calories from Fat

Portabella Beans

Portabella mushrooms are now widely available, and a good thing it is, for nothing compares with their hearty, meaty flavor. Though I first made this as a side dish for plain roasted chicken, I found it also made a wonderful midnight snack over a piece of baguette.

$\frac{1}{2}$ pound portabella mushrooms
$\frac{1}{4}$ cup minced shallots
1 cup white wine
1$\frac{1}{2}$ teaspoons minced fresh thyme (or $\frac{1}{2}$ teaspoon dried)
1 can (19 ounces) white beans, drained (2 cups)
Salt
Freshly ground black pepper

1. Wipe the mushrooms clean and cut the caps and stems into strips.

2. Heat a nonstick skillet for 30 seconds and add the mushrooms, stirring constantly. Cook for 2 minutes and then add the shallots and wine. Sprinkle thyme over all and let the mushroom mixture simmer for 10 minutes.

3. Add the beans and, gently stirring, heat through. Add salt to taste. Serve with pepper ground on top.

4 SERVINGS
PER SERVING: 214 Calories • 0.6 Gram Fat • 3.1% Calories from Fat

Braised Fennel

This was the recipe that made me like fennel for the first time, though now I enjoy it in many other guises, as well. A hearty dish, it's good with mashed potatoes to soak up the delicious gravy.

2 fennel bulbs
1 medium onion, chopped
1 garlic clove, minced

2 cups nonfat beef broth
1 teaspoon minced fresh parsley

1. Cut the stems and leaves off the fennel bulbs and discard. Slice the fennel bulbs in half lengthwise.
2. Coat a nonstick skillet with cooking spray and heat for 30 seconds. Add the onion and fennel, cut side down, and brown them for about 5 minutes, or until the bottom of the fennel starts to get some color. Add the garlic and brown for 1 minute more.
3. Carefully add the beef broth and bring to a boil. Reduce the heat, cover, and simmer for 20 minutes, or until the fennel is very tender. Serve hot, sprinkled with the fresh parsley.

4 SERVINGS
PER SERVING: 43 Calories • 0.2 Gram Fat • 2.9% Calories from Fat

Fennel and Pears

The intriguing licorice taste of fennel is pared with the sweet taste of stewed pears, highlighted by tarragon.

1 large fennel bulb
$\frac{2}{3}$ cup chicken bouillon
$\frac{1}{2}$ medium onion, minced

1 medium pear, chopped
$\frac{3}{4}$ teaspoon minced fresh tarragon
(or $\frac{1}{4}$ teaspoon dried)

1. Chop the stalks of the fennel bulb. Cut the bulb into quarters and thinly slice each quarter.
2. Place the fennel slices with the remaining ingredients in a skillet and bring the mixture to a boil. Reduce the heat, cover, and simmer for 15 minutes, or until the fennel is soft. Serve warm or at room temperature.

4 SERVINGS
PER SERVING: 42 Calories • 0.3 Gram Fat • 6.0% Calories from Fat

Baked Onion Apple

A plain roasted turkey or chicken breast will be deliciously enhanced by this savory side dish.

2 Granny Smith apples
$\frac{1}{4}$ cup chopped onion
1 tablespoon maple syrup
$\frac{1}{8}$ teaspoon powdered sage

1. Preheat the oven to 450°F.

2. Cut the apples in half and carefully remove the core. In a small mixing bowl, combine the onions, syrup, and sage and distribute this stuffing evenly over the four apple halves.

3. Arrange the apples stuffing side up on a glass plate in ¼ inch of water in a baking dish. Bake for 30 minutes, or until the apples are soft when pierced.

4 SERVINGS
PER SERVING: 46 Calories • 0.1 Gram Fat • 1.7% Calories from Fat

Sweet Potato Parsnip Puree

Purees don't need added fat to be full of flavor and satisfying, as this version amply proves. Complement the beautiful orange hue with a deep green vegetable for a lovely looking plate.

1 pound sweet potatoes
2 parsnips
3 cups water
2 garlic cloves, chopped
1 small onion, chopped
2 bay leaves
1 teaspoon minced fresh rosemary (or ½ teaspoon dried)
1 teaspoon Dijon mustard
Salt and freshly ground black pepper
1 tablespoon minced fresh parsley

1. Scrub the sweet potatoes and parsnips and cut into chunks. Place them with the water, garlic, onion, bay leaves, and rosemary in a medium-size saucepan and bring to a boil. Reduce the heat, cover, and simmer for 20 minutes, or until the vegetables are soft.

2. Drain the vegetables and remove the bay leaves. Cool slightly. In a food processor with a steel blade or a blender, puree the vegetables in a few batches. Return the puree to the saucepan, add the mustard, and heat through on very low heat, stirring to avoid scorching. Add salt and pepper to taste. Sprinkle with the parsley and serve hot.

6 SERVINGS
PER SERVING: 94 Calories • 0.4 Gram Fat • 3.7% Calories from Fat

Mashed Parsley Parsnips

This is an adaptation of a recipe my friend David has contributed to Thanksgiving celebrations quite a few times. It's always a hit.

3 medium parsnips
1 garlic clove, peeled
$\frac{1}{4}$ cup minced parsley
Salt and freshly ground black pepper
2 teaspoons grated Parmesan cheese

1. Preheat oven to 350°F.
2. Peel the parsnips and cut them into 1-inch chunks. Place the parsnips and the garlic clove in a saucepan and cover with water. Bring to a boil, reduce the heat, and simmer for 20 minutes, or until the parsnips are soft.
3. Drain the parsnips and garlic and mash with a potato masher. Do not use a food processor or blender. Mix in the parsley and add salt and pepper to taste. Place the mixture in a ovenproof dish and sprinkle with the Parmesan cheese. Bake for 15 minutes.

6 SERVINGS
PER SERVING: 52 Calories • 0.4 Gram Fat • 7.1% Calories from Fat

Elisa's Potato Chips

My dear friend Elisa makes these treats all the time. We've had them for breakfast, lunch, dinner, and late-night snacks; we've sprinkled all sorts of spices on them; and we've dipped them in all sorts of sauces and dips. And every time we marvel: These are so good!

4 medium potatoes
$\frac{1}{2}$ teaspoon olive oil
Salt and freshly ground black pepper

1. Preheat the oven to 375°F. Rub the olive oil over two nonstick baking sheets.
2. Scrub the potatoes, but don't peel them. Slice them thinly into rounds, about 6 to the inch. Lay them in a single layer on the baking sheets and bake for 15 minutes.
3. Turn them over and bake for 20 more minutes, or until nicely browned and puffed. Add salt and pepper to taste. Serve and eat immediately.

4 SERVINGS
PER SERVING: 71 Calories • 0.6 Gram Fat • 7.9% Calories from Fat

Potatoes with Fresh Broccoli Rabe

My mother made this often in Holland, and now you can now eat it, too—and you don't even have to be able to ask for "raapsteeltjes stamppot." Reuse the water in the recipe as directed to preserve nutrients.

4 medium potatoes
2 cups broccoli rabe
$\frac{1}{3}$ cup skim milk
1 tablespoon grated Parmesan cheese
Freshly ground black pepper

1. Cut the potatoes into chunks and boil or steam them for about 15 minutes, or until they're soft.

2. Meanwhile, place the water into a food processor or blender, add a few leaves of broccoli rabe, and puree. Add a few more leaves and puree again. When you're unable to puree any further, place a colander over a bowl and drain the puree. Spoon the puree into a separate bowl, pour the green broth back into the blender, and continue pureeing the rest of the broccoli rabe. Do this as often as necessary until all the broccoli rabe has been pureed. (Use the green broth as a base for soup; it's chock-full of vitamins and minerals.)

3. Combine the cooked potatoes in a mixing bowl with the milk and Parmesan cheese. Mash with a potato masher. Add the drained broccoli rabe puree, and mix well. Serve immediately with pepper to taste on top.

4 SERVINGS
PER SERVING: 84 Calories • 0.6 Gram Fat • 5.8% Calories from Fat

Pesto Potatoes

All the goodness of stuffed potatoes and none of the guilt: Milk and roasted garlic give you the creamy satisfaction and basil gives you a blast of taste.

4 baking potatoes
$\frac{1}{4}$ cup chopped Vidalia onion
1 garlic clove, roasted
3 tablespoons skim milk
$\frac{1}{4}$ cup fresh basil leaves
1 teaspoon vegetable-broth mix
Salt and freshly ground black pepper
1 tablespoon grated Parmesan cheese

1. Preheat the oven to 400°F.

2. With a fork, prick the potatoes all over and place them on a baking sheet. Bake for 1 hour, or until cooked. Remove the potatoes and let them cool enough to handle them. Lower the oven to 350°F.

3. In a food processor or blender, place the onion, garlic, milk, basil, and broth mix. Process and scrape down until all the ingredients are minced. Place the onion-basil mixture in a large mixing bowl.

4. When the potatoes have sufficiently cooled, cut a thin slice from the top and scoop out the flesh, keeping the shells intact. Place the potato flesh in the mixing bowl with the onion-basil mixture. Using a potato masher, thoroughly blend the potatoes and the onion-basil mixture. Add salt and pepper to taste.

5. Spoon the potato mixture back into the shells and sprinkle with the Parmesan. Arrange the stuffed shells on the baking sheet and bake for 20 minutes, or until heated through.

4 SERVINGS
PER SERVING: 107 Calories • 0.6 Gram Fat • 4.6% Calories from Fat

New Potatoes in Dill Sauce

Tender young potatoes paired with fresh dill create a delightful companion dish to steamed fish or grilled chicken. If the new potatoes are very small, you might not even need to cut them at all, though you will need more than two potatoes per person.

6 medium new potatoes, diced
$\frac{1}{2}$ cup water
$\frac{1}{2}$ cup skim milk
1 tablespoon all-purpose flour
1 shallot
1 teaspoon vegetable-broth mix
2 teaspoons minced fresh dill

1. Place a vegetable steamer in a saucepan and add water up to the bottom of the basket. Add the potatoes, cover, and steam until cooked, about 15 minutes.

2. Meanwhile, slowly heat a large nonstick skillet. In a food processor or blender, combine the water, milk, flour, shallot, broth mix, and 1 teaspoon of the dill. Process. Pour the mixture into the warm skillet and, stirring constantly, bring it to a boil. Boil for 3 minutes.

3. Place the potatoes in a serving bowl, pour the sauce over, and mix well. Sprinkle with the remaining dill. Serve hot.

4 SERVINGS
PER SERVINGS: 123 Calories • 0.2 Gram Fat • 1.6% Calories from Fat

Garlic Parmesan Mashed Potatoes

Very few dishes are as comforting as mashed potatoes. I generally don't peel my potatoes and consequently end up with skins in my mashed potatoes, but I happen not to care. If you like yours nice and smooth, by all means peel your spuds before you steam them.

4 medium potatoes
4 garlic cloves
$\frac{1}{2}$ cup skim milk
$\frac{1}{4}$ teaspoon salt
2 teaspoons grated Parmesan cheese
Freshly ground black pepper

1. Cut the potatoes into 2-inch chunks. Peel the skins off the garlic, but leave the bulbs whole.

2. Place a vegetable steamer in a saucepan and add water up to the bottom of the basket. Add the potatoes and place the garlic on the top. Cover tightly and steam the potatoes for 15 minutes, or until very soft.

3. Remove the steamed garlic and mash very well with a fork. Set aside. Mash the potatoes, garlic, milk, salt, and Parmesan with a potato masher. Stir in the mashed garlic. Serve hot immediately, with pepper to taste on top.

4 SERVINGS
PER SERVING: 85 Calories • 0.4 Gram Fat • 4.1% Calories from Fat

Roots with Vegetable Sauce

This is an archetypal recipe, devised by my friend Elisa. I have eaten it often, and it's never the same twice. Elisa just picks the best vegetables she can find, steams them, blends some of them with a bit of the steaming liquid and seasonings, and dinner is served. For this book I had to come up with a definitive version, but it represents a small universe of possibilities.

1 large garnet yam
2 potatoes
3 parsnips
1 medium onion
$\frac{3}{4}$ teaspoon anise seed
1 teaspoon honey
1 teaspoon light miso
$\frac{1}{2}$ teaspoon salt
2 teaspoons tahini

1. Cut the yams, potatoes, parsnips, and onion into chunks. Place a vegetable steamer in a saucepan and add water up to the bottom of the basket. Add the vegetable chunks, cover tightly, and steam for about 15 to 20 minutes, or until they're tender.

2. Place 2 cups of the vegetables and ¾ cup of the steaming liquid in a food processor or blender. Add the anise, honey, miso, salt, and tahini. Puree.

3. Serve the vegetables in a warmed bowl, with the pureed sauce on the side.

4 SERVINGS
PER SERVING: 206 Calories • 1.9 Grams Fat • 8.2% Calories from Fat

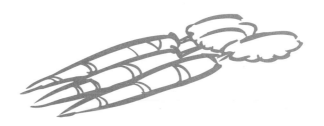

Filled Sweet Potatoes

Sweet, creamy, and satisfying without the added fat calories from the usual toppings. If you're in a hurry, mash all the ingredients and serve them in a bowl instead of in their skins. The presentation will be less elegant, but the taste will still be delicious.

2 large sweet potatoes
1 tablespoon maple syrup
1 teaspoon lemon juice
$1\frac{1}{2}$ teaspoons minced fresh thyme (or $\frac{1}{2}$ teaspoon dried)
$\frac{1}{4}$ teaspoon freshly ground black pepper

1. Preheat the oven to 350°F.

2. Scrub the potatoes and pierce them a few times with a fork. Place them on a baking sheet and bake for 45 minutes, or until they're soft when pierced.

3. Reduce the heat to 300°F.

4. Let the potatoes cool slightly. Cut them in half lengthwise, and carefully scoop out as much of the flesh as you can, leaving the shell intact.

5. In a medium-size mixing bowl, mash the sweet-potato flesh with the maple syrup, lemon juice, thyme, and pepper. When thoroughly mixed, carefully fill the empty shells with the sweet-potato mixture. Do not mash down too hard. Place the shells back on the baking sheet and return them to the oven for 15 minutes, heating through.

4 SERVINGS
PER SERVING: 63 Calories • 0.2 Gram Fat • 2.3% Calories from Fat

Baked Potato with Creamed Spinach

For me, creamed spinach is comfort food, and during difficult spells I have eaten it three times a week or more. It nourishes me in a very special way. Whether or not it does anything for you emotionally, you'll find it delicious.

4 large baking potatoes
1 package (10 ounces) frozen chopped spinach, thawed
1 cup skim milk
4 tablespoons all-purpose flour
1 small garlic clove
1 scallion
1 tablespoon vegetable-broth mix
2 teaspoons minced fresh thyme (or 1 teaspoon dried)
Salt and freshly ground black pepper

1. Heat the oven to 400°F.

2. Scrub the potatoes and pierce all over with a fork. Arrange them on a baking sheet and bake for 50 to 60 minutes, depending on how large the potato is, or until they're soft when pierced with a skewer.

3. Place the thawed spinach in a colander to drain. Squeeze the spinach with your hands to get out the last bit of liquid.

4. Place the milk, flour, garlic, scallion, broth mix, and thyme in a food processor or blender. Heat a nonstick skillet for 30 seconds. Process the milk mixture until smooth and pour immediately into the hot pan. Stir constantly until the sauce thickens.

5. Add the drained spinach and stir into the sauce. Cook, stirring constantly, for 5 minutes. Add salt and pepper to taste.

6. Place the baked potatoes on individual serving plates. Cut a long slit into the top and push open slightly. Spoon the creamed spinach into the opening and over the rest of the potato. Eat while hot.

4 SERVINGS
PER SERVING: 168 Calories • 0.6 Gram Fat • 2.9% Calories from Fat

Acorn Squash Rosemary Puree

Deep orange and aromatic, this puree could also easily be flavored with other herbs, such as thyme or basil.

1 medium acorn squash
½ cup skim milk
2 shallots, chopped
1 garlic clove, finely minced
1 tablespoon vegetable-broth mix
1 teaspoon minced fresh rosemary (or ½ teaspoon dried)
¼ teaspoon dried sage
¼ teaspoon chili powder
Salt and freshly ground black pepper
2 teaspoons minced fresh parsley

1. Preheat the oven to 375°F.

2. Cut the squash in half and remove the seeds with a spoon or a butter curler, if you happen to have one. Place the halves cut side down on a baking sheet with a high rim. Pull the rack out of the oven and place the baking sheet on it. Pour water around the squash to about a ½-inch depth. Push in the rack very gently so the water doesn't slosh and bake for 30 minutes, or until the squash is soft when pierced with a wooden skewer. Let cool.

3. Scoop out the squash flesh and place into a large bowl. Discard the skins. With a potato masher, puree the flesh.

4. In a medium-size saucepan, heat the skim milk, shallots, garlic, vegetable-broth mix, rosemary, sage, and chili powder. When the milk mixture is hot, add the squash puree and heat through, stirring continuously. Add salt and pepper to taste. Serve in a preheated bowl and sprinkle with the parsley just before serving.

4 SERVINGS
PER SERVING: 65 Calories • 0.2 Gram Fat • 2.9% Calories from Fat

Vegetable Barley

This is a hearty combination of starch and vegetable, which you can serve warm as a main meal or cold as a salad.

2 cups tomato puree
2 cups water
1 cup barley
1 medium sweet red pepper, chopped
1 medium onion, chopped
2 garlic cloves, minced
1 tablespoon low-sodium soy sauce
1 tablespoon fresh oregano
2 bay leaves
$\frac{1}{2}$ cup frozen peas

1. In a medium-size saucepan, combine the water and tomato puree. Stir.

2. Add the barley, pepper, onion, garlic, soy sauce, oregano, and bay leaves and bring to a boil. Reduce the heat and simmer for 45 minutes. Mix in the frozen peas and heat through. Serve hot.

4 SERVINGS
PER SERVING: 249 Calories • 1.5 Grams Fat • 5.2% Calories from Fat

CHAPTER 5

DESSERTS

For me, dinner just isn't complete without a bit of dessert. It's that final sweet morsel that tells my brain and body that I have eaten and am satisfied. If I plan a dessert, I'm less tempted to snack and I eat less. Knowing that a delicious dessert awaits me makes other sacrifices much easier.

Coming up with desserts that meet the 10-percent-of-calories-from-fat standard is a challenge. In examining these recipes, look for what is present, not for what is missing. They're neither skimpy nor wimpy, and they're most definitely not lacking in sweetness. (Their fat content may be virtuous, but I haven't skimped on sweeteners.) If weight loss is an urgent goal, I advise you to take the calorie content into account. My main concern here has been fat percentage and I assume you understand that even when you cut fat way down, it doesn't mean the calories from other sources are negligible!

The desserts in this chapter go from simple, homey comfort foods, to haute cuisine. Chocolate Almond Coconut Pudding and Baked Apples are good for weekday night, family fare. These are also foods I personally like to make extras of: Just knowing they're waiting in the refrigerator, in case I feel like snacking, makes it easier to give up high fat foods at other times.

Tailor your dessert so that it complements your dinner, especially when you entertain. For example, a curry meal needs a cool dessert with a novel taste, and Rosewater Cardamon Rice Pudding is perfect. Consider ending a spicy, heavier meal with a Piña Colada Freeze. Ginger Clove Ginger Bread and Banana Lemon Bread are great with an after-dinner cup of tea, or they can be dressed up with any number of different nonfat ice creams and nonfat frozen yogurts currently available. Meringue with Raspberries makes a totally elegant finish to a gourmet meal.

Angelic Cake with Raspberries

Because I incorporated a little baking powder, this isn't a true angel food cake. But the resulting taste won't disappoint even the most discriminating baker.

$\frac{1}{2}$ cup all-purpose flour
$\frac{1}{2}$ cup sugar
$\frac{1}{4}$ teaspoon baking powder
$\frac{1}{4}$ cup pasteurized dried egg whites
$\frac{3}{4}$ cup water
$\frac{1}{2}$ teaspoon vanilla extract
$\frac{1}{2}$ teaspoon almond extract
10 ounces fresh raspberries

1. Preheat the oven to 375°F. Have a 10-inch springform pan ready. Line the bottom of the pan with parchment.

2. In a medium-size bowl, sift together the flour, sugar, and baking powder.

3. In a large bowl, mix together the egg whites, water, and the extracts. Beat the egg whites with an electric beater until they're stiff and peak when you pull the beaters out.

4. Combine the flour mixture with the egg whites one large spoonful at a time, incorporating the flour with long strokes. When all the flour is incorporated, pour and scrape the mixture into the springform pan and gently flatten out the top. Bake for 30 minutes. Let the cake cool for 10 minutes. Cut around the edge and release the spring. Remove the cake from the pan and let it cool completely. Serve with whole raspberries, or puree and strain raspberries and then spoon the sauce over cake slices.

6 SERVINGS
PER SERVING: 140 Calories • 0.4 Gram Fat • 2.2% Calories from Fat

Banana Lemon Cake

Mashing bananas is easiest with a potato masher. If you have children helping you, this is a particularly good job to give them, though we all know that for the very best mashed bananas, the initial mashing must be done with scrupulously clean small hands.

$\frac{1}{2}$ cup unsweetened applesauce
1 cup brown sugar
1 teaspoon lemon juice
1 teaspoon vanilla extract
$\frac{1}{2}$ teaspoon grated lemon zest
$1\frac{1}{2}$ cups mashed ripe bananas
2 cups all-purpose flour
1 teaspoon baking powder
$\frac{1}{2}$ teaspoon baking soda
$\frac{1}{2}$ cup cornmeal
$1\frac{1}{2}$ cups nonfat vanilla yogurt cheese (page 8)

1. Preheat the oven to 350°F. Coat a nonstick 9 by 9-inch baking pan with cooking spray. In a large mixing bowl, combine the applesauce, brown sugar, lemon juice, vanilla, and lemon zest. Add the mashed bananas and mix well.

2. In a medium-size mixing bowl, sift together the flour, baking powder, and baking soda. Add the cornmeal and stir well.

3. Add the flour mixture to the banana mixture in three batches, stirring well after each addition. Pour the batter into the prepared pan and bake for 45 minutes. Let the cake cool for 5 minutes before turning it out of the pan. Finish cooling.

4. Top with vanilla yogurt cheese and serve.

12 SERVINGS
PER SERVING: 187 Calories • 0.4 Gram Fat • 2.1% Calories from Fat

Ginger Clove Gingerbread

I always put cloves in my gingerbread because it brings back memories of the goodies I ate as a child in Holland. The crystallized ginger brings this bread up to date.

$1\frac{1}{2}$ cups all-purpose flour

4 teaspoons pasteurized dried egg whites

1 teaspoon baking soda

$\frac{1}{4}$ teaspoon baking powder

1 teaspoon ground ginger

$\frac{1}{4}$ teaspoon ground cloves

$\frac{1}{4}$ teaspoon ground cinnamon

$\frac{1}{4}$ teaspoon mace

1 tablespoon finely chopped crystallized ginger

$\frac{1}{3}$ cup unsweetened applesauce

$\frac{1}{3}$ cup maple syrup

$\frac{1}{3}$ cup brown sugar

$\frac{1}{3}$ cup water

$\frac{1}{2}$ teaspoon apple-cider vinegar

1. Preheat the oven to 300°F. Coat a nonstick 9 by 9-inch baking pan with cooking spray.

2. Sift the flour, pasteurized dried egg whites, baking soda, baking powder, ginger, cloves, cinnamon, and mace into a medium-size mixing bowl. After sifting, stir with a whisk to combine the spices well. Add the chopped ginger and stir in. Be sure the ginger pieces are well separated and incorporated evenly into the flour.

3. In a separate mixing bowl, combine the applesauce, maple syrup, brown sugar, water, and vinegar. Add the liquid ingredients to the flour mixture and combine lightly but well, using long strokes. Pour the batter into the prepared pan immediately and bake for 25 minutes, or until a wooden skewer inserted near the center comes out clean.

4. Let the gingerbread cool in the pan for 10 minutes before removing to cool completely.

9 SERVINGS
PER SERVING: 136 Calories • 0.3 Gram Fat • 1.9% Calories from Fat

Peach Bread Pudding

Bread pudding is a comfort food, and paired with ripe, juicy peaches, you'll never miss the fat of the traditional variety. You can use day-old challah, French bread, whole-wheat bread, or a combination of different breads.

5 cups bread cubes

1½ cups fresh peach slices

1 cup skim milk

¼ cup brown sugar

2 egg whites (or 4 teaspoons pasteurized dried egg whites plus 2 tablespoons water)

¾ teaspoon vanilla extract

½ teaspoon coriander

¼ teaspoon mace

1. Preheat the oven to 350°F. Coat a 1½-quart ceramic baking dish with cooking spray.
2. In a large mixing bowl, combine the bread cubes and peaches.
3. In a separate mixing bowl, combine the milk, sugar, egg whites (or pasteurized dried egg whites and water), vanilla, coriander, and mace. Mix well. Add the liquid mixture to the bread cubes and peaches and combine gently. Pour into the prepared baking dish.
4. Place the baking dish on a baking sheet with high sides in the oven and add enough water to the baking sheet so the baking dish sits in 1 inch of water. Bake for 1 hour. Serve hot or warm.

6 SERVINGS

PER SERVING: 220 Calories • 1.1 Grams Fat • 4.4% Calories from Fat

Rosewater Cardamom Rice Pudding

This rice pudding get its flavors from India and is a cousin to kheer. You can get rosewater in Indian grocery stores or order it from the Hancock Shaker Village in Pittsfield, Massachusetts.

$1\frac{1}{2}$ cups water
1 cup basmati rice
1 pinch of saffron threads
$\frac{1}{2}$ cup evaporated skim milk
1 teaspoon rosewater
$\frac{1}{4}$ teaspoon almond extract
$\frac{1}{4}$ teaspoon cardamom
$1\frac{1}{2}$ tablespoons brown sugar

1. Bring the water, rice, and saffron threads to a boil in a medium-size saucepan. Cover, reduce the heat, and simmer for 20 minutes, or until the rice is very soft.

2. Add the milk, rosewater, almond extract, cardamom, and brown sugar. Simmer, stirring constantly, for 5 minutes. Serve warm or at room temperature.

6 SERVINGS
PER SERVING: 139 Calories • 0.2 Gram Fat • 1.3% Calories from Fat

Cranberry Applesauce

There is no comparison between homemade applesauce and a commercial product. This version is just as great with some slices of cold turkey as it is for dessert. Try it on top of nonfat vanilla frozen yogurt.

4 apples
2 tablespoons water
$\frac{1}{3}$ cup cranberries

2 tablespoons honey
$\frac{1}{2}$ teaspoon ground cinnamon
$\frac{1}{4}$ teaspoon ground cloves

1. Peel, core, and chop the apples.

2. Place all the ingredients in a saucepan and bring to a boil.

3. Reduce the heat and simmer, stirring occasionally, for 15 minutes. If you like your applesauce sweeter, add some sugar. Serve hot, warm, or cold.

4 SERVINGS
PER SERVING: 112 Calories • 0.5 Gram Fat • 3.7% Calories from Fat

Chocolate Almond Coconut Pudding

This pudding is absolutely delicious, creamy, sweet, and filled with flavor. No one will suspect it is low fat!

$\frac{1}{3}$ cup unsweetened cocoa
$\frac{1}{2}$ cup sugar
3 tablespoons cornstarch
$2\frac{1}{2}$ cups skim milk
1 teaspoon vanilla extract
$\frac{1}{2}$ teaspoon almond extract
$\frac{1}{4}$ teaspoon coconut extract
1 tablespoon almond slivers

1. Sift the unsweetened cocoa, sugar, and cornstarch into a medium-size saucepan and mix thoroughly. Whisk in the milk. Measure the extracts into a separate cup and set aside.

2. Heat the mixture over medium heat, whisking constantly. When the mixture thickens and boils, add the extracts and continue whisking. Reduce the heat to low and let the pudding boil for 1 minute. Remove from the heat and immediately pour into a serving bowl.

3. Let the pudding cool for 10 minutes. Then cover the bowl with plastic wrap to prevent a skin from forming and cool to room temperature. You may serve it at room temperature or cold. Sprinkle with the almonds just before serving.

4 SERVINGS
PER SERVING: 205 Calories • 2.4 Grams Fat • 10.0% Calories from Fat

Caramel Tapioca Pudding with Bananas

This tapioca pudding has the creamy satisfaction I often crave after a meal with a lot of fresh vegetables. The hint of caramel comes from the brown sugar and the evaporated milk. You may substitute other fruits, but in this version, bananas are my favorite. Be sure to use quick-cooking tapioca.

$\frac{1}{2}$ cup evaporated skim milk

1$\frac{1}{4}$ cups water

3 tablespoons quick-cooking tapioca

2 tablespoons brown sugar

$\frac{1}{4}$ teaspoon vanilla extract

Pinch of salt

1 ripe banana, sliced

1. In a medium-size saucepan, combine the evaporated milk, water, tapioca, brown sugar, vanilla, and salt. Bring to a boil while stirring. Reduce the heat and simmer the pudding for 5 minutes, stirring constantly.
2. Pour the pudding into a bowl. Add the sliced bananas and mix. Serve at room temperature or chill and serve cold.

6 SERVINGS
PER SERVING: 56 Calories • 0.1 Gram Fat • 1.6% Calories from Fat

Piña Colada Freeze

The recipe is for one serving, but you can multiply the ingredients as you need to, adjusting the coconut extract to taste. This is the perfect thing to spoon and sip on a hot summer night.

1 ripe banana

1 cup nonfat vanilla yogurt cheese (page 8)

1 pineapple ring, drained

$\frac{1}{4}$ teaspoon coconut extract

1. Peel the banana, cut it into 1-inch chunks, and freeze it in a freezer bag for at least 3 hours.
2. Place the yogurt cheese, frozen banana chunks, and drained pineapple ring in a food processor or blender. Process until the banana chunks are blended. Serve immediately in tall chilled glass with a straw and a long spoon.

1 SERVING
PER SERVING: 291 Calories • 0.8 Gram Fat • 2.2% Calories from Fat

Strawberry Banana Sorbet

You can vary the berries and juice concentrate and make endless new variations. Try mango and white grape juice, raspberries and cranberry juice, or papaya and pineapple juice. The bananas give this its creamy base, so don't omit them.

2 ripe bananas
$\frac{1}{3}$ cup frozen concentrate apple juice, undiluted
$1\frac{1}{2}$ cups strawberries, frozen
Mint leaves

1. Peel the bananas, cut them into 1-inch chunks, and put them in the freezer until the chunks are solid (about 30 minutes, depending on your freezer).

2. Combine the apple-juice concentrate in a food processor or blender, with a few of the banana chunks and process. Keep adding the fruits a little at the time and process until smooth. With the motor off, push down the fruits with a spatula.

3. Serve immediately in chilled glass bowls and garnish with the mint leaves.

4 SERVINGS
PER SERVING: 89 Calories • 0.5 Gram Fat • 4.4% Calories from Fat

Noodle Kugel

Sweet kugel is a wonderful comfort food. This dessert is, after chicken soup, the best healer of aching bodies and souls.

$\frac{1}{8}$ teaspoon olive oil
6 ounces noodles
3 egg whites, whipped (or 2 tablespoons pasteurized dried
egg whites plus 6 tablespoons water, whipped)
$\frac{1}{2}$ cup skim milk
$\frac{1}{4}$ cup chopped dried apples
$\frac{1}{4}$ cup golden raisins
$\frac{1}{4}$ cup brown sugar
1 teaspoon vanilla extract
$\frac{1}{4}$ teaspoon almond extract

1. Preheat the oven to 350°F. Spread the olive oil on the inside of an ovenproof casserole dish.

2. Cook the noodles according to package directions; do not overcook. In a mixing bowl, lightly combine the noodles and remaining ingredients. Pour the noodle mixture into the prepared baking dish and bake uncovered for 35 minutes.

4 SERVINGS
PER SERVING: 262 Calories • 2.0 Grams Fat • 7.0% Calories from Fat

Meringues with Raspberries

Every cook comes across at least one recipe that scares her or him. Meringues were mine. But these are truly easy, and they will work. Do not try making meringues on humid days, and be sure all your equipment is absolutely free of grease. One of the great things about using pasteurized dried egg whites is that you don't need to be afraid that a speck of fatty egg yolk will ruin the dish.

$\frac{1}{4}$ cup powdered sugar
$\frac{1}{4}$ cup granulated sugar
$\frac{1}{8}$ teaspoon cream of tartar
2 tablespoons pasteurized dried egg whites
6 tablespoons water
1 package (10 ounces) raspberries in syrup
1 teaspoon cornstarch

1. Preheat the oven to 200°F. Line a baking sheet with parchment. In a small mixing bowl, combine the two sugars and cream of tartar.

2. In a stainless-steel bowl, place the pasteurized dried egg whites and water. Mix them well, using the end of a spoon to break down the larger clumps. (You won't get a totally smooth liquid, but if you skip this step and use the electric mixer right away, you'll make a little egg white "cloud.")

3. Insert clean beaters into an electric mixer and whip up the egg whites. When foamy, start adding the sugar mixture a spoonful at the time while running the machine. Keep beating the egg whites until stiff peaks form when you pull the beaters away from the meringue.

4. Drop one-sixth of the beaten egg white on the parchment. With the back of a spoon make a hollow in the middle and gently build up the edges. Repeat so that you have 6 "nests." Bake for 2 hours. Then turn off the oven and let the meringues sit for another hour. During this process *do not open the oven to peek!*

5. Meanwhile, defrost the raspberries, drain gently, and reserve ¾ cup of the juice. Place one tablespoon of reserved juice in a cup and add the cornstarch. Mix well. Place the rest of the reserved juice in a small saucepan. With a small whisk, thoroughly blend the cornstarch into the raspberry juice until the juice looks milky and no clumps remain. Heat over low to medium heat, stirring constantly. When the mixture starts to thicken, keep whisking and boil for 1 minute. Let the sauce cool.

6. When you're ready to assemble the dessert, place the meringue shells on individual serving plates. Spoon the raspberries onto the shell, and pour the sauce over all. Serve immediately.

6 SERVINGS
PER SERVING: 104 Calories • 0.1 Gram Fat • 0.5% Calories from Fat

Dutch Cookies

The flavor of these cookies reminds me of the treats baked in Holland around Sinterklaas time (December 5). These soft cookies smell heavenly and, despite a bit of egg yolk, are still very low in fat.

2 cups all-purpose flour
$\frac{1}{2}$ cup sugar
1 teaspoon baking soda
2 teaspoons pasteurized dried egg whites
$\frac{1}{2}$ teaspoon ground cinnamon
$\frac{1}{4}$ teaspoon ground cloves
$\frac{1}{8}$ teaspoon ground nutmeg
$\frac{1}{4}$ teaspoon mace
$\frac{1}{2}$ cup honey
1 egg, whole
2 tablespoons water
1 teaspoon powdered sugar

1. Preheat the oven to 350°F. Coat nonstick cookie sheets with cooking spray.

2. In a large bowl, sift together the flour, sugar, baking soda, pasteurized dried egg whites, cinnamon, cloves, nutmeg, and mace.

3. In a small mixing bowl combine the honey, egg, and the water. Mix the flour mixture into the honey mixture and stir vigorously until a dough forms.

4. Flour your hands, pinch off a small piece of dough, and make a walnut-size ball. Continue, placing the balls 2 inches apart on the prepared cookie sheets.

5. Bake for about 8 minutes, or until the bottoms of the cookies start to brown. Remove from the cookie sheets immediately and cool. Sprinkle with the powdered sugar.

28 COOKIES
PER COOKIE: 68 Calories • 0.3 Gram Fat • 3.3% Calories from Fat

Pears in Cassis

Though this will work with any combination of frozen berries, be sure to include the ripe pears. For an extra treat, serve with a generous scoop of nonfat frozen vanilla yogurt.

2 pears
1 cup frozen strawberries
1 cup frozen blueberries
8 tablespoons creme de cassis

1. Preheat the oven to 350°F. Slice the pears in half and scoop out the core. Place the halves in individual ovenproof dishes, core side up.

2. In a medium-size bowl, combine the frozen berries. Dollop one-quarter of the berries into the hollow of each pear. Sprinkle the remaining berries over all.

3. Pour 2 tablespoons of creme de cassis over each pear half. Cover the dishes with aluminum foil and crimp closed. Bake for 30 minutes. Let the pears sit covered for 10 minutes before serving. Serve hot or warm.

4 SERVINGS
PER SERVING: 245 Calories • 0.9 Gram Fat • 3.6% Calories from Fat

Fried Bananas

I scheduled testing for this recipe early in the morning, and so I ate these for breakfast at 5:00 A.M. I highly recommend it. Then again, I would probably highly recommend these at any time, day or night. If you omit the brown sugar, they can even be a side dish for a curry meal.

4 ripe bananas, peeled
½ teaspoon butter

2 tablespoons brown sugar
Dash of cinnamon

1. Slice the bananas in half lengthwise. (The easiest technique is to lay them flat on a cutting board and carefully slice them lengthwise with a very sharp knife, holding the banana down with the palm of your hand.)

2. In a nonstick skillet, melt the butter over low to medium heat. Place the banana in the pan, cut side down, and fry until slightly brown on the bottom.

3. With a wide spatula, turn the bananas over. Sprinkle the brown sugar over the top and add a little cinnamon. Continue frying until the reverse sides are also brown.

4 SERVINGS
PER SERVING: 89 Calories • 0.8 Gram Fat • 7.7% Calories from Fat

Apple Cobbler

Comforting, filling, warm, and sweet: It doesn't get much better! This dessert is wonderful with nonfat vanilla yogurt. You can also substitute pears for the apples when they're good and ripe. If you don't have Granny Smith apples available, use sweet apples with lemon juice sprinkled over them.

$\frac{1}{8}$ teaspoon canola oil

6 medium Granny Smith apples

$\frac{1}{4}$ cup currants

$\frac{1}{2}$ teaspoon cinnamon

$\frac{1}{4}$ teaspoon cloves

$\frac{1}{8}$ teaspoon nutmeg

1 cup skim milk

$\frac{3}{4}$ cup whole-wheat flour

$\frac{1}{3}$ cup brown sugar

2 teaspoons baking powder

$\frac{1}{2}$ teaspoon almond extract

1. Preheat the oven to 350°F. Pour the oil in the bottom of an 1½ quart baking dish with a rim at least 1½ inches high, and spread the oil all around with your fingers.

2. Peel the apples if their skins don't look appetizing. Otherwise, skip this step. Quarter and core the apples and slice each quarter into 3 slices. Evenly arrange the apples in the baking dish. Sprinkle the currants over all.

3. In a small mixing bowl, whisk the cinnamon, cloves, and nutmeg. Set aside.

4. In a food processor or blender, combine the milk, flour, sugar, baking powder, and almond extract. Process until smooth and pour over the apples. Take the spice blend and sprinkle over the batter.

5. Bake for 35 minutes, or until nicely browned on top. Serve immediately.

6 SERVINGS
PER SERVING: 178 Calories • 0.6 Gram Fat • 3.1% Calories from Fat

DESSERTS

Baked Apples with Maple Syrup

These baked apple halves are easier to make than trying to core out a whole apple. Just a few minutes' worth of work, and the irresistible aroma of baking apples, cinnamon, and cloves will fill your house.

4 large apples
$\frac{1}{3}$ cup maple syrup
$\frac{1}{4}$ teaspoon ground cinnamon
$\frac{1}{4}$ teaspoon ground cloves
$\frac{1}{4}$ cup golden raisins

1. Preheat the oven to 350°F. Slice the apples in half and scoop out the core. Place snugly in a baking dish, sides touching and hollowed side up. Pour ½ inch of water into the baking dish, but avoid getting water into the hollows of the apples.

2. In a small mixing bowl, combine the maple syrup, cinnamon, and cloves. Spoon the mixture into the hollows of the apples. Sprinkle the raisins evenly over the apples.

3. Bake for 35 to 45 minutes, or until the apples are totally soft when pierced. Eat hot.

4 SERVINGS
PER SERVING: 172 Calories • 0.6 Gram Fat • 2.9% Calories from Fat

Baked Peaches with Vanilla Ice Cream

When peaches are ripe, this is what you want to serve for dessert. You get all the intense flavor of the hot peaches in contrast with the smooth coolness of the ice cream. Heavenly!

4 ripe peaches
$\frac{1}{2}$ cup apple juice
2 tablespoons brown sugar
$\frac{1}{4}$ teaspoon ground cloves
$\frac{1}{2}$ teaspoon vanilla extract
4 scoops nonfat vanilla ice cream

1. Preheat the oven to 350°F. Slice the peaches in half and remove the pits.
2. Pour the apple juice in an ovenproof dish. Place the peaches, cut side up, side by side in the dish.
3. In a small bowl, combine the brown sugar, cloves, and vanilla. Spoon the sugar mixture into the cavities left by the pit. Cover the dish with aluminum foil and crimp the sides. Bake for 30 minutes.
4. To serve, dollop a scoop of ice cream on a plate with two peach halves.

4 SERVINGS
PER SERVING: 151 Calories • 0.1 Gram Fat • 0.7% Calories from Fat

INDEX